# POLICING
## *for*
# PROFIT

*Exposing Corruption Between
Police, Courts and
Corporations*

BY

BARBARA ORBAN

ISBN: 978-0-692-64883-4
Copyright © 2016 by Barbara Orban

# ACKNOWLEDGMENTS

My story would not be possible without the knowledge, expertise, and dedication to the public among a group of Tampa, Florida police officers. As I began to have questions about some perverse practices used by the Tampa Police Department to generate "extra income," in particular traffic ticket fraud, these considerate, principled men in blue provided answers. They taught me how to prove Tampa's ticket and arrest quotas, as well as why quotas can lead to fraud. In my federal lawsuit that attempted to eliminate these quotas (and some related illegal practices), these officers were willing (and some even eager) to testify about the problem in order to have these practices remedied on behalf of the public. As a caveat, one key police informant told me the information he was providing could be framed so as to disparage police officers. He said he was entrusting me to use the information meaningfully and substantively, thereby *not* disparaging the profession of law enforcement. I have done so. My final chapters explain police officers were not the problem. I express my sincere appreciation and respect to these Tampa police professionals who chose to "protect and serve" our community.

Further, I am most thankful to Robert Merkle, the former U.S. Attorney for the Middle District of Florida, who agreed to have his firm represent me over a traffic ticket, only because I alleged and documented police fraud. This appreciation also includes his law partner, Joseph Magri, likewise a former federal prosecutor, who identified the laws and legal theories that established 11 Tampa Police Department practices were illegal and unconstitutional, thereby providing the legal foundation for my federal lawsuit against the City of Tampa that attempted to eliminate their policing for profit tactics.

In addition, it is great to be a professor, as one is surrounded by highly intelligent and astute colleagues and friends. As I looked to find motivations for many perverse behaviors (cause-and-effect), in some cases it was a colleague who found and conveyed to me the likely reason. I greatly value working with people who possess such exceptional curiosity and insight. Their focus on the public's welfare is important, recognizing we do work in a College of "Public" Health. In particular, I thank Professors Etienne Pracht and John Large for their interest, effort, and collegiality, as we have ventured to tell the truth about red-light traffic cameras, thereby challenging powerful proprietary interests—quite a formidable undertaking.

I also greatly appreciate the friends, co-workers and graduate students who provided their personal experiences with Tampa police ticket fraud for use in my federal lawsuit, which included a U.S. Air Force Captain. They shared their personal knowledge in the interest of the public.

I am most grateful to my book editor, Willy Mathes, who has skillfully guided me throughout the book writing journey, which has more steps involved than a novice book writer would expect. Additionally, he has linked me with the many other professional experts needed to successfully publish a book.

Finally, I thank my family, who have been supportive of my interest in the policing for profit subject since the year 2000, recognizing this is a long time. They have offered their own examples from various sources, as well as provided advice on my approach to addressing the problem. They (no doubt, against their will) have become experts on the topic—which includes identifying great locales for a speed trap—proving family is the best!

*"…it is time for a sober reassessment of the power we have concentrated in the hands of prosecutors and the alarming absence of effective checks and balances to prevent the widespread abuse of that power. Perhaps the telltale sign of the seriousness of the situation is the law school textbook, Prosecutorial Misconduct, now in its second edition. In an honest criminal justice system, there would be no need for such a textbook."*

Arnold I. Burns
Deputy U.S. Attorney General from 1986-1988
*The Wall Street Journal,* 1998

# TABLE OF CONTENTS

Prologue ..................................................................................... 9

Chapter 1    Why Police Abandon "Community Policing" .............. 11
             *(a.k.a. "To Protect and Serve")*

Chapter 2    Adopting a "Business Approach" to Policing .............. 17
             *(i.e., "To Collect and Serve")*

Chapter 3    Ticket Quotas ................................................. 31
             *Using Police Officers to Generate Revenue*

Chapter 4    Arrest Quotas ................................................. 43
             *Deciding in Advance How Many People Must Be Jailed*

Chapter 5    Home Rule ...................................................... 55
             *An Excuse for Public Officials to Twist the Law*

Chapter 6    Kangaroo Courts ............................................... 65
             *Where Everyone Is Guilty, But Given Their Day in Court*

Chapter 7    The Proprietary Traffic Safety Establishment .......... 81
             *The Auto Insurance Industry*

Chapter 8    The Proprietary Public Safety Establishment ........... 95
             *Other Corporate Interests*

Chapter 9    My Federal Kangaroo Court Experience ................. 105
             *A Tale of Falsities and Omissions*

Chapter 10   Case-Fixing ..................................................... 125
             *Why You Can't Beat City Hall*

Chapter 11   The Federal Appellate Court ........................... 139
             *Reversing the Outcome, While Pretending Not To*

Chapter 12   The Surprising Nexus of Policing
             for Profit in Tampa, Florida ............................ 149

Chapter 13   Reasons Why the U.S.
             Is the Incarceration Nation ............................. 157

Appendix A   Tampa Police Investigation of a
             White Officer Killing a Black Teenager ........... 167

Appendix B   My Proposed Settlement Agreement
             (Federal Lawsuit) with the City of Tampa ...... 175

Appendix C   GAO Analysis Disclosing Price Fixing
             by Insurance Companies ................................ 185

# PROLOGUE

Many law enforcement officials, agencies and judges exhibit honesty, integrity, and professionalism. They deserve commendation for their focus on the public and their safety. My story is *not* about them. Instead, my story reveals that some law enforcement officials, agencies and judges lack integrity and professionalism, and some are outright dishonest. This occurs from a lack of credible accountability systems within the justice system. Accountability systems must be improved, such as exist for other professions; while imperfect, these systems are better than nothing.

In particular, my tale reveals how some police officials abuse their power by using tactics to generate revenue from tickets, arrests and property seizures, which is known as "policing for profit." The goal of policing for profit is to produce more and more money for self-serving purposes: for example, larger salaries, benefits, police equipment, and new facilities. However, it encourages fraud, because in this enterprise, the end is more important than the means.

The notion that revenue growth is a good thing comes from the private sector, where such growth is a symbol of success, whether on Wall Street or Main Street U.S.A. Meanwhile, there are many private corporations that rely on law enforcement growth to achieve their own growth. Some law enforcement agencies willingly partner with these private enterprises to create expense for the public, while ignoring their mission is public service.

In contrast to the private sector, "value" is the hallmark of success in the public sector, which focuses on being effective, while also efficient (containing costs). In the public sector, continuous revenue growth is generally viewed as contrary to staying focused on value and public service.

Based on my personal account of law enforcement and judicial practices in one major metropolitan city where policing for profit practices are well documented, one fact is painfully clear: improved accountability systems are unquestionably needed to protect the public from public officials, agencies and judges who are greedy, dishonest, or incompetent, or who partner (sometimes covertly) with special interests. It is time to make meaningful improvements to the so-called "justice system." I learned this first-hand from living in Tampa, Florida, where policing for profit was rolled out in 1999.

# CHAPTER 1

# WHY POLICE ABANDON "COMMUNITY POLICING"

## (a.k.a. "To Protect and Serve")

*"In Chief Holder's term, there was this community stabilization and relationship-building. And then Chief Hogue was able to expand on the relationships, but with a business model to reduce crime."*

John Bennett
Assistant Police Chief
Tampa, Florida, 2009

I witnessed a disturbing transformation when community policing was abandoned by the Tampa (Florida) Police Department and replaced with a "business approach," also known as policing for profit. The change began in 1999 and was fully implemented by 2004. The transition was actually transparent in 1999 since, quite abruptly, officers started working in packs (called "wolf packs") to create speed traps throughout Tampa. Sometimes, they would change speed limit signs, lowering the speed limit, and then run a speed trap until drivers became aware of the new speed. They regularly targeted the local interstate, even though crashes were infrequent, meaning the multitude of tickets was not about preventing crashes.

In 1999, Tampa's population was about 300,000. With "community policing," the Tampa police produced about 24,000 arrests and 50,000 traffic tickets annually. When the "business approach" was fully adopted in 2004, arrests nearly doubled and tickets tripled (45,000 arrests and 145,000 tickets annually). The arrest increase was reported in a "miscellaneous" category of crime that was not counted in violent or non-violent crime statistics, presumably because the Tampa police were *simultaneously* posturing that violent and non-violent crime rates had decreased (even though twice as many people were arrested for committing a crime). By 2005, the Tampa police "business approach" created about 190,000 court cases annually, which was one court case per every 1.7 Tampa residents. Business was booming for the Tampa Police Department and the local court!

Simply stated, the business approach to law enforcement emphasizes revenue generation from tickets and arrests, as well as property seizures from citizens, in order to aggrandize police and court budgets. The larger budgets have been used to pay higher salaries, benefits, and bonuses for police administrators; to purchase more equipment, including military equipment; to acquire nicer facilities; and to hire more officers in order to generate more tickets, arrests, and property seizures. This business approach is cyclic, where revenue growth begets further growth—fueling an ever-expanding "justice" system. Growth in tickets and arrests necessitates larger police departments and the need for more attorneys and judges to manage the larger caseloads, as well as expanding jails and prisons. It is based on a Wall Street private sector model, in which revenue growth is a hallmark of success and rewarded accordingly.

My personal interest in the Tampa Police Department's "business model" resulted from being a victim of traffic ticket fraud in both 1999 and 2000. These are my only tickets in 45 years of driving, and both were dismissed in court by proving the police officer was untruthful. To understand why an officer would take the time to fabricate a traffic offense, as it is a waste of time and marginalizes the police profession, I queried officers in my neighborhood and learned the Tampa Police Department was transitioning from "community policing" to a "business approach" that emphasized ticket quotas for the purpose of revenue generation (money). With the business approach, each officer's annual evaluation rated them on the number of moving violation tickets issued relative to a quota. Underachievers were put in a remediation program where their ticket productivity was measured more frequently, and they were at risk for being fired if not meeting expectations. A number of officers I spoke with said they did not approve of quotas and did not understand why police administrators suddenly wanted so many traffic tickets.

I searched for a rationale for the tickets and found what motivated Tampa police administrators to develop ticket quotas. It was greed! Since the 1950s, a Florida tax on auto insurance (0.85%) has been paid in each municipality, accruing to the municipality's police pension. It is called Chapter 185 revenue and is the State's contribution to police pensions in its municipalities.[1] Florida law was changed in 1999 to reward police with "extra" pension benefits if they increased Chapter 185 revenue, which is achieved by boosting auto insurance rates paid by residents in their municipality. Florida law was amended such that annual Chapter 185 revenue collected in excess of the amount collected in 1997 must be used for "extra" police pension benefits. In 1999, the Florida legislature and Governor Jeb Bush allowed this to become law, meaning State law incentivized policing for profit by linking the financial interests of municipal police administrators with auto insurance companies. Effectively, they became business partners. At the time, points on a driver's license from a single traffic ticket were estimated to increase a driver's premium by 80% to 95% for a period of three to seven years. Given "carte blanche" by the State to go full steam ahead with this arrangement, Tampa police administrators used ticket quotas to create large auto insurance increases, in order to secure "extra" pension benefits for themselves.

---

1  Chapter 185 of the Florida Statutes is titled "Municipal Police Pensions."

It should be noted, during the 1990s auto insurance rates paid in Tampa, and throughout Florida, were stagnant due to the great strides in motor vehicle safety achieved from the public health sector, which happens to be my discipline. Then, in the 10 years following 1999, Tampa drivers paid $1 billion more in auto insurance relative to the 1990s, in part, due to Tampa's ticket quotas. Of this $1 billion, $8 million accrued to the Tampa police pension for "extra" pension benefits. One could say Tampa police administrators sold-out rather cheaply, getting less than 1% of the $1 billion insurance increase they helped to create. The graph below illustrates the increase in their Chapter 185 collections.

**Tampa's Chapter 185 Premium Tax Revenues**

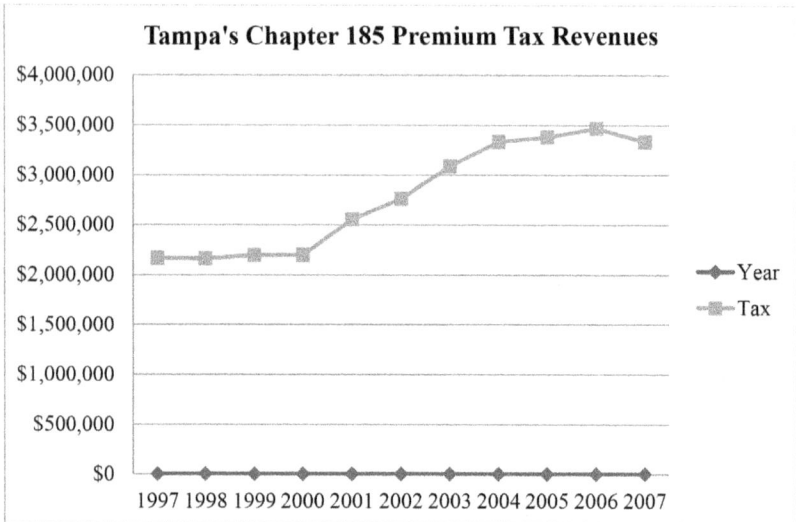

Policing for profit, however, ultimately allowed the Tampa police to nearly *double* their pension benefits through a combination of large salary increases and a 40% pension benefit increase that was approved by the Florida legislature in 2004, which occurred after auto insurance premiums paid in Tampa had increased by 40%. To illustrate the large pension increase, one can compare the pensions of Police Chief Bennie Holder, who retired in 2003—before the salary and pension benefit increases—and Police Chief Stephen Hogue, who retired in 2009, after the large salary and pension increases.

Chief Holder's annual pension is $65,000, whereas Chief Hogue's annual pension is $126,000, which is 94% more than the pension of Chief Holder.

In Tampa, it is now possible for police officers to retire in less than 30 years with a pension equivalent to their full salary at the time of retirement—a rich reward for running the police department like a private enterprise. Some officers will actually receive their full salary in annual pension benefits for more years than they worked for the Tampa Police Department.

Meanwhile, experienced patrol officers explained to me why they opposed traffic ticket quotas. In order to write tickets, they need to hide somewhere, awaiting an infraction, because their marked cars are deterrents to violations. They explained they prefer to respond to calls for service or be highly visible patrolling problem areas, instead of hiding to write traffic tickets. In other words, they cared more about "protecting and serving." Further, they believed Tampa's traffic squads should manage traffic problem areas, since it is all they do and they use unmarked vehicles. The officers also said quotas encourage ticketing minor violations that do not impact public safety, since the goal becomes achieving the quota to get a good evaluation, rather than focusing on reducing crashes. In their view, because ticketing minor violations does not impact public safety, it signals to the public the motivation is money, which marginalizes the role of police officers and creates an adversarial relationship with the public. The officers also believed a written warning system should be used for minor or moderate offenses, which allows officers to educate drivers, absent the costs of a ticket (fine and potential auto insurance increase). Further, they expressed concern that new officers might actually believe simply writing large numbers of tickets is a genuine measure of police effectiveness.

As such, my personal story is not about "rogue" police officers. Instead, it is about honest police officers who had no ability to influence policies from Tampa police and city administrators who emphasized policing for profit. The officers gave me inside information to help me prove Tampa's perverse policies, in order to change them. Since I am a professor, they initially assumed I would publish their information. However, a credible publication outlet did not exist and the supporting evidence was somewhat limited. Instead, I filed a federal lawsuit in 2004 attempting to halt Tampa's ticket quotas, because I was a victim of ticket fraud due to Tampa's quotas.

Many Tampa officers were willing to testify in court, since they wanted the quotas eliminated. Further, I had about a dozen upstanding individuals who would testify they also were victims of Tampa police traffic ticket fraud. My lawsuit also allowed for deposing officials who were advancing policing for profit, thereby documenting the problem. In addition, my lawsuit attempted to end Florida's kickback law between auto insurers and "extra" police pension benefits. This kickback law conflicted with another State law and a federal court ruling that made it illegal for public officials to personally profit from money generated in their role as public officials, such as a judge collecting a percentage of fines assessed.

From my federal case, I learned accountability systems do not exist for the court, as the federal judges' rulings included falsities and major omissions, yet the judges faced no consequences. More astounding, the federal judges engaged in untruths that blocked my case from being heard by a jury where officers, other victims, and I would have testified about Tampa's quotas that resulted in fraud. The appellate judges' untruths also assured my case would not be heard by the U.S. Supreme Court, which might have overturned their ruling, if truth were told, thereby allowing my case to proceed to a jury trial. One of my attorneys explained that if my case was heard by a jury, the entire criminal justice system would be called into question. It *does* need to be called into question, as demonstrated by my experience and evidence.

The problems and opportunities for improvement of the justice system are explained herein, often using Tampa, Florida as an example of how the present system can run amok under the current lack of accountability.

# CHAPTER 2

# ADOPTING A "BUSINESS APPROACH" TO LAW ENFORCEMENT

## (i.e., "To Collect and Serve")

*"It's a results-oriented process today, fairness be damned."*
Robert Merkle
Former U.S. Attorney for the Middle District of Florida
1998

Following my second experience with traffic ticket fraud in 2000, Robert Merkle, the former U.S. Attorney for the Middle District of Florida, agreed to have his firm represent me after I explained my situation to him. His tenure as U.S. Attorney had addressed public corruption. Mr. Merkle sent four county commissioners to prison for racketeering. He also investigated the local State Attorney over case-fixing, so he clearly understood how courts can be rigged to produce a desired outcome.

Mr. Merkle agreed to meet with me and discuss my traffic ticket, since I alleged police fraud. I explained to him that, following a minor traffic accident that had mitigating circumstances and resulted in a dented license plate, a Tampa police officer told me I had not violated a traffic law, but his supervisor had nonetheless ordered a ticket. This occurred even though Florida law did not require a police investigation of my minor, non-injury crash. The officer further explained my insurance company wanted the ticket issued, and the State of Florida required the ticket issued for my insurance company. He also suggested I file a lawsuit against the State. A second officer, a rookie (trainee), who wrote the crash report, told me during a follow-up phone call that he had fabricated information on the report because these reports are written per "police policy" and not based on an investigation. Unbeknownst to me, the false report was used as *ex parte* (secret) evidence in court, despite Florida law banning the use of crash reports in court.[2]

The officers' statements were baffling, so I queried Tampa's Internal Affairs Bureau (IAB) about their practices. An IAB detective said the officers could make up anything, since the police department wanted a conviction on the ticket, regardless of whether or not I had violated a traffic law. The detective further explained that no agency would intervene about the fabrications. I asked Mr. Merkle if this was true: "Are the police allowed to fabricate charges and evidence to advance convictions?"

He paused and then responded, saying, "You would not want to know all the things police officers make up."

Mr. Merkle was a principle-driven attorney, and had been quoted in the book, *The Tyranny of Good Intentions: How Prosecutors and Bureaucrats Are Trampling the Constitution In the Name of Justice.* In it, he explained that "bogus cases" are being prosecuted to get the statistics needed to justify prosecutorial budgets. The problem does not appear to originate with "rogue" police officers or judges, but

---

2  I was granted a new hearing and my ticket was dismissed. However, I still experienced a nearly $4,000 auto insurance increase due to the false crash report. My insurance company offered to refund the money if the crash report errors and omissions were corrected; however, Tampa's police attorney (Kirby Rainsberger) refused to make corrections, despite admitting the report had errors. He contended the police write too many reports to engage in disputes about their accuracy and suggested settling any differences in court.

rather it comes from their administrators who tolerate or even encourage dishonest practices to advance a "business approach" to law enforcement—one that emphasizes arrest and conviction statistics for the purpose of generating revenue, which is growth that advances the need for larger agencies and courts. Meanwhile, "bogus cases" have far greater consequences than traffic ticket fraud.

Throughout the U.S., Innocence Commissions have worked to reverse judgments against innocent persons who were wrongly convicted of crimes that resulted in the death penalty. In addition to exonerations from DNA evidence, some convictions have been reversed because evidence had been falsified, fabricated or ignored. The need for accountability systems to prevent this from continuing was explained in Jon B. Gould's book *The Innocence Commission: Preventing Wrongful Convictions and Restoring the Criminal Justice System.*

Gould wrote: *To refuse or stonewall, to blindly defend the criminal justice process, without being open to new, best practices, is to dishonor the oath that many of us took as officers of the court, the law, or the state. Criminal justice is a profession. It is time that we started treating it as one.*[3]

When John Bennett was promoted to Tampa's Assistant Police Chief in 2009, he explained the "business approach" in a news story, clarifying differences between Tampa's former police chief (Chief Bennie Holder) and the current chief (Chief Stephen Hogue). Bennett said, *"In Chief Holder's term, there was this community stabilization and relationship-building. And then Chief Hogue was able to expand on the relationships, but with a business model to reduce crime."* Tampa's business model added arrest quotas to the ticket quotas, while also increasing the ticket quota, which ultimately required more citizens to hire attorneys, pay fines and court costs, and possibly be sentenced to jail or prison or have their property seized.

---

3  Gould further explained: *"Other professions in America, most notably transportation and medicine, routinely convene review bodies to learn from errors. It is embarrassing, and should be unacceptable, that the legal and criminal justice fields largely do not... It is time for leaders in law and criminal justice to follow the example of their peers in transportation and medicine and undertake a systematic review of errors."*

In my federal lawsuit that attempted to ban Tampa's ticket quotas and the kick-back between auto insurers and "extra" police pension benefits, John Bennett used the word *business* 13 times in his deposition when describing Tampa's approach toward crime. Bennett explained the focus was on *accountability* and said, "*All of those things have lent itself to more production, which whether you're in the private sector or the public sector is what everybody wants.*" Bennett believed the Tampa Police Department was running a business that produces arrests and tickets, and increasing productivity of arrests and tickets is "*what everybody wants*" as an accountability measure, similar to the private sector where increasing productivity is positive. Meanwhile, Tampa's quotas were leading to fraud and enormous auto insurance increases, which is *unwanted* "productivity" from the public's perspective.

Policing for profit is the *opposite* of community policing, which focuses on the public's welfare and safety. The difference in priorities is evidenced when SWAT teams raid the homes of alleged small-time drug dealers, putting the homeowner at risk for injury or death from the SWAT team, over a suspected minor crime. With the business approach, the opportunity to make an arrest or seize the house as police property (for drug dealing) takes precedence over the homeowner's safety, which would be a main consideration with community policing.

For example, in 2014, the Tampa police SWAT team raided a home after a police informant alleged the occupant (a renter) had sold $160 of marijuana from the house in recent months and was also involved in selling heroin.[4] The Tampa police knew the renter owned a gun at the time they raided the house. The SWAT team shot and killed the man upon entering his bedroom, since he was armed with his gun. The fact is, Florida's *Stand Your Ground* law allows residents to shoot intruders who come into their home. How would this man know the intruders were a police SWAT team when pointing a gun at his bedroom door, anticipating an intruder, only to be promptly shot dead by expert marksmen? The paid police informant,

---

4  Police property seizures can occur for crimes, such as drug dealing, even if the property is owned by someone else who did not participate in the crime.

who alleged the man was selling marijuana and heroin, was a drug addict and criminal, and later admitted he lied about the heroin sales for the purpose of getting paid by the police. Experts later criticized the Tampa Police Department for not securing evidence (audio or video) of heroin being sold at the house before raiding it. Tampa's Internal Affairs Bureau (IAB) investigation nonetheless absolved the officers of the shooting, because "they feared for their lives." The IAB never investigated the supervisor's reckless use of the SWAT team in creating hazardous circumstances that resulted in the man's death, even after finding only $2 worth of marijuana and no evidence of heroin in the man's home. Regardless, Tampa's police chief, Jane Castor, publicly defended the raid and shooting, which is a form of posturing called "circling the wagons."

Unfortunately, existing accountability systems allow the police to investigate themselves whenever and however they want. Internal Affairs Bureaus are actually "risk management" departments. Disciplining any officer for untruthfulness, incompetence, or putting a citizen at unnecessary risk would provide evidence against the police to advance a lawsuit or settlement with the victim or their family. Therefore, police departments have a financial incentive to posture, such that any incompetence or untruthfulness is not egregious, as evidenced by Internal Affairs investigations typically justifying police shootings, because the officer "feared for his life," absent any analysis of whether the officer unnecessarily or through incompetence created circumstances that caused their fear. A lack of professionalism in law enforcement is encouraged when untruthfulness, incompetence, poor decision-making, or recklessness is whitewashed in IAB investigations.

Policing for profit may have actually precipitated the 2014 shooting in Ferguson, Missouri that resulted in prolonged, nationwide protests after a white police officer shot an unarmed black teenager. The officer had stopped the teen for walking in the street, despite the road having minimal traffic, which is a minor offense at best, but a possible opportunity to generate revenue from writing a ticket or making an arrest if an outstanding warrant exists. The teen leaned into the patrol car and had a scuffle with the officer. The officer shot him in the hand, contending the teenager was reaching for his gun. Then, the teenager ran away from the officer. The officer clearly did not fear for his life, since he was sitting in his patrol car with his gun and the teenager was running away. The officer had choices. He could call for back-up, while pursuing the young man in his vehicle. In theory, he could have approached the teenager using non-lethal force; however, the officer did not have a Taser, because (he said later) he found it inconvenient to carry on his belt. If apprehended under either of these scenarios, the teenager would have been able to explain what occurred that resulted in the officer shooting his hand. A jury would then decide who to believe, assuming the teenager was charged with a crime and the stories differed. Instead, the officer got out of his vehicle and shot the teenager multiple times, killing him. First, the officer shot him for running away. Then, he shot him for coming back—a "no win" situation for the teenager.

In the days that followed, the widespread public protests attempted to assure independent officials would conduct a credible investigation of the officer's conscious decision to leave his vehicle and shoot the teenager, acting as judge, jury and executioner, despite not being in harm's way.

The Ferguson demonstrators sought accountability from public officials, a scene played out by other frustrated communities across the nation. Likewise, a similar police shooting took place in Tampa, where a whitewashing of police incompetence and untruthfulness occurred. In December 2000, a white rookie officer shot and killed a black teenager who was sitting in a stolen SUV, which subsequently led to some local protesting. The protesting was quashed after a Tampa police spokesman reported, "*The officer does not have the luxury of trying to walk away*" and claimed the teenager had a sawed-off shotgun, implying the officer acted in fear of this gun. Tampa's police attorney, Kirby Rainsberger, conducted the Internal Affairs investigation, which took more than a year to produce. The IAB report concluded the rookie did *not* abide by police policy, which required him to stay under the cover of his own patrol car until the vehicle occupants were removed. Further, a B-B gun (not a sawed-off shotgun) was found under the seat *after* the shooting, meaning the police spokesperson had misrepresented circumstances to the media. More importantly, the rookie's recounting of events was contradicted by physical evidence. He claimed to stand adjacent to the driver, with the driver's door open, and then shot the teenager when the SUV started to roll, fearing for his life from being stuck down by the door. However, the analysis of gun powder residue suggested the rookie was *not* standing at such close range, discrediting the rookie's rationale for shooting the teenager.

The rookie received only a *reprimand*, despite: a) not abiding by Tampa police policy (SOP 831: Vehicle Stops—Felony/High Risk), b) creating the circumstances, contrary to SOP 831, that resulted in the teen's death, and c) claiming circumstances that were refuted by physical evidence, suggesting the rookie was untruthful. The Notice of Disciplinary Action did not mention that the rookie's violation of policy resulted in the death of a teenager.[5,6] This was the same rookie who nine months earlier told me he had fabricated information on my crash report. From my perspective, by training him to make false entries on crash reports, they were conditioning him for larger fabrications.

The local State Attorney in Tampa concluded the rookie's shooting was justified, because the officer feared for his life. Apparently, the State Attorney was similarly disinterested that the rookie's sworn

---

5   Appendix A provides the Notice of Disciplinary Action, followed by Rainsberger's 5-page IAB investigation.

6   Some police chiefs do set higher standards than evidenced in Tampa. For example, in 2014, the interim police chief of St. Petersburg, Florida fired a white rookie police officer after he shot an unarmed black teenager in the head, rendering the teen permanently disabled from a brain injury. The teenager was in a stolen truck and began to drive away. The officer claimed to "fear for his life" as the truck was driving toward him. However, the shots hit the passenger side and back windows only, contradicting the rookie's story. His use of force was deemed unjustified. The mother of the teenager is suing the City and police department.

statement was inconsistent with physical evidence or that he violated police policy. I called the State Attorney's office after his decision was reported and explained the rookie had been untruthful based on my experience with him. The woman with whom I spoke was Pam Bondi, who is now Florida's Attorney General. She explained the State Attorney does not have to account for how his decision was made, which reveals another failure of the justice system in assuring accountability. From my perspective, Tampa had a "good old boy" network in place, where the Tampa Police Department and State Attorney jointly allowed a rookie officer to continue testifying in court, despite the circumstances that resulted in the teenager's death.

*Why did the State Attorney not at least ban the rookie from testifying in court as a police officer, since his statement was not consistent with the physical evidence?* This would send a message to the Tampa Police Department and other local law enforcement agencies that truthfulness is expected. Instead, truthfulness and competence did not seem to matter.

While police agencies posture to the public that the state or district attorney provides "outside investigations" into police shootings or misbehavior, this assumption is flawed. Instead, state and district attorneys are partners with the police in prosecuting cases. If discrediting an officer for misbehavior, particularly if it results in the officer's termination, then all court cases in which the officer is involved are put in jeopardy for prosecutors. For example, a Tampa DUI squad sergeant was terminated in 2014 after a local newspaper revealed he participated in setting up the DUI arrest of an attorney with the help of personnel from attorneys of an opposing law firm during a high profile court case. This triggered a federal investigation, and also forced the State Attorney to reconsider all DUI arrests involving the sergeant. Many charges were dropped, including the DUI charge against the attorney who was set up.

Prior to filing my federal lawsuit, I called the State Attorney's office a second time to complain that the Tampa Police Department had a written policy that required officers to engage in a "color of law" crime, which is a felony. Tampa's written policy required officers to write traffic tickets in traffic crash investigations, even after the officer concluded probable cause did not exist, which resulted in the need for officers to fabricate information on the crash report to justify issuing the ticket. It turned out the rookie's explanation of his fabrications in my case were actually required by the Tampa Police Department. The State Attorney staffer responded that they prosecute cases *with* the Tampa police and do not prosecute police officers. The woman did not want further information. In other words, advancing convictions took precedence over expectations for truthfulness, affirming Mr. Merkle's statement: *It's a results oriented process today, fairness by damned.*

To improve accountability, police and prosecutor investigations should consider not only whether the officer feared for his life, but also whether the officer or his/her supervisor created or contributed to the circumstances that led to this fear. If their own unsound actions contributed to their fear, then the officer or supervisor should be sanctioned. Merely contending an officer "feared" for his or her life is setting the standard too low. More importantly, an expectation of truthfulness must be held as nothing less than essential. As my case and further examples will show, the Tampa police and local court tolerate untruthfulness among public officials. However, when Tampa police administrators want to fire an officer, there are at least two documented cases demonstrating they will use any untruthfulness as a basis for termination.

Further, "qualified immunity" for law enforcement officers should be abandoned and replaced with an accountability system parallel to state medical boards. Qualified immunity protects officers from liability (lawsuits), *if* the officer exercised his or her responsibilities reasonably. However, "reasonably" has been defined by agencies to include fearing for one's life when shooting and killing someone, *regardless of the circumstances*, which is too low a standard. Instead, states should be required to have law enforcement boards that review complaints from citizens, similar to medical boards. For example, if a surgeon accidentally kills a patient by nicking an artery, they are not charged with murder. Instead, a family member of the victim files a complaint with the state medical board, which decides whether or not prevailing standards of practice were met. If standards were not met, sanctions occur, for example a fine, continuing education, and/or suspension or revocation of the physician's license, depending on the gravity of the deviation from the standard of care. Also, findings from this state review can be used in any related civil lawsuit. Similarly, a state law enforcement board should respond to complaints, with all complaints and findings becoming a public record, similar to medical boards. Also, similar to state medical boards where the maximum penalty is revocation of a medical license, the maximum penalty for police officers should be decertification in law enforcement. Public agencies have sovereign immunity, which limits the payout to a victim, such that incompetent officers should not be allowed to shield themselves using qualified immunity, especially since sovereign immunity protects a jurisdiction from excessive payouts.

At present, when court rulings are based on false, fabricated or ignored evidence, the court rulings can only be appealed to a higher court. Meanwhile, the law enforcement officer, prosecutor or judge who misrepresented or ignored facts faces no consequences for doing so, indicating the need for accountability systems for such officials.

To make matters worse, attorneys are deemed "unethical" by state bar associations if criticizing a judge's ruling, even if the judge ignored facts or misrepresented evidence. Consequently, bar associations force attorneys to act as though they are in *The Emperor's New Clothes*, only permitted to see a "great outfit" for all court rulings. The present accountability system, developed by attorneys (the appellate process), simply creates more jobs for attorneys. An additional accountability system is needed whereby an independent entity investigates complaints that allege a prosecutor or judge ignored, falsified or misrepresented facts in any court case, and should not be restricted to demonstrating that a pattern of practice exists or conducted solely as an "internal" investigation. If failing to differentiate facts from fiction, officials should be counseled or sanctioned, and ultimately removed if a pattern exists, recognizing the root cause can be ignorance, incompetence, laziness, corruption, maliciousness, or senility.

Finally, allowing attorneys to criticize court rulings without penalizing them would advance accountability among prosecutors and judges. It is unethical and should be illegal for state bar associations to silence attorneys who believe a prosecutor or judge ignored facts or misrepresented evidence. When I complained about the perverse Tampa police policies (fabricating tickets and crash reports) to the Florida Department of Law Enforcement (FDLE), a special agent advised on obtaining the policies in writing. After City of Tampa officials ignored my complaint about their written policies, an FDLE supervisor explained to me the best means to address Tampa's perverse policies was through the media. Despite the importance of the media, attorneys are not permitted to address their concerns about a judge's ruling with the media. The media is an outlet for dissent, but attorneys are prohibited from using it with regard to a judge's ruling.

As an example, in my federal lawsuit, I sought changes to require Tampa police policies to conform with State law, alleging 11 police policies and practices were illegal and unconstitutional. My case went to mediation twice, such that the policy changes I sought were detailed in a proposed settlement agreement. However, attorneys for the City of Tampa fabricated that I sought "prospective relief," meaning the police would be prohibited from investigating or enforcing any laws regarding me and my family, which would be foolish and preposterous to seek. This was one of many untruths made by attorneys for the City of Tampa, but they were never criticized by the federal judges for their fabricating such in court filings.

The City's external counsel, John Makholm, wrote the following in a court filing, "*Dr. Orban is requesting Federal intervention to 'enjoin' members of a municipal police department essentially, from contacting her (and presumably her husband and other family members who have gotten tickets) in the future. In essence she is requesting a special dispensation, a shield if you will from prospective police investigation/*

*enforcement in the future."* Mr. Makholm attended the first mediation where my settlement agreement was submitted, so he had personal knowledge his statement was untrue.[7] Instead of criticizing or sanctioning Mr. Makholm for making this false statement, Judge Steven D. Merryday, and later three elderly federal appellate judges in Atlanta (Gerald Bard Tjoflat, R. Lanier Anderson, and Susan H. Black) pretended in their rulings that I actually sought prospective relief, even though the declarations in my lawsuit and my proposed settlement agreement affirm this is false. In their ruling to dismiss my lawsuit, the federal appellate judges wrote the following: *Dr. Orban is no more entitled to prospective relief than any other citizen of Tampa.* This calls into question the extent to which court rulings are based on facts versus fiction.

The three appellate judges also misrepresented that I was "guilty" on the traffic ticket, even though my ticket had been dismissed. Their false statements about guilt, as well as my purportedly seeking prospective relief, assured that any appeal I might make to the U.S. Supreme Court would not be heard. Thereby, the three senior federal appellate judges engaged in falsities to assure my evidence would never be heard by a jury, where experienced Tampa police officers would testify about ticket and arrest quotas, as well as the secret submission of false crash reports to court hearings. In addition, the judges' fabrications were disparaging to my attorney, since they suggest he attempted to secure prospective relief for me after I was found guilty on a traffic ticket. Nonetheless, my attorney must remain silent, as he could be sanctioned by the Florida Bar if providing documentation to the media that the federal district and appellate judges' statements were untrue.

Attorneys must have their First Amendment rights restored to advance accountability of court rulings, which I believe will help deter the police-court partnership. Judges would be less likely to

---

7   Appendix B provides my proposed settlement agreement. Since attorneys for the City of Tampa were untruthful in their court filings about what I sought, I can reveal what was proposed.

partner with the police (repeating falsities or fabrications) if attorneys could openly disagree and provide facts to the media—the court of public opinion.

At present, judges have given themselves *prospective relief*, as they have enjoined attorneys from criticizing them: a special dispensation, a shield, if you will, from *the truth*.

## CHAPTER 3

# TICKET QUOTAS

## Using Police Officers to
## Generate Revenue

*"What is a quota system? Where we tell officers you got to write 30 tickets a year or 30 tickets a month or 30 tickets a day, and that's what you got to turn in. It's illegal. It's been ruled in the courts that it's illegal to have quotas, and I would be willing to bet you there's not a police officer in Florida who doesn't know that . . . No major says you got to write this many tickets, I guarantee you that because that's a quota, but there is some expectation that officers do their job, which a part of that job is writing traffic citations and enforcing traffic laws . . . If they don't do their job, then, yes, they probably are rated below expectations or unsatisfactory."*

Deposition of Tampa Police Chief Stephen Hogue
October 26, 2005

Quotas are essential to policing for profit, but problematic for the public, since officers may need to fabricate or force infractions in order to achieve the number needed to get a good evaluation. For example, in Waldo, Florida (population 1,015), the speed limit on the main road would vary, going up and down, for the purpose of ticketing drivers who missed the lower speed limit sign. In 2014, Waldo's police chief resigned after officers complained to the City Council about the town's ticket quotas, triggering an investigation from the Florida Department of Law Enforcement. For decades, the small town was known as a speed trap. In 2013, Waldo's seven police officers wrote nearly 12,000 traffic tickets to out-of-town drivers, about 1,700 tickets per officer. Waldo's police department was subsequently disbanded and the local sheriff assumed responsibility for the town.

In his deposition in my federal lawsuit, Tampa's Police Chief Stephen Hogue explained that quotas are illegal. Nonetheless, he allowed his officers to be informed of the number of tickets and arrests needed for a good performance evaluation, under the pretense they were "expectations" and not a quota. It was doubletalk. Quotas were called expectations to avoid the appearance of an illegal practice.

The Tampa Police Department had three traffic ticket quotas, all of which were documented in the annual performance evaluations of its officers. The quotas were: 1) traffic squad quota, 2) patrol officer quota, and 3) ticket-at-every-crash quota (even if the officer believes probable cause did not exist to write a ticket and including minor non-injury crashes that did not require a police investigation). The quotas generated revenue from fines and created large auto insurance increases, which resulted in "extra" police pension benefits.[8]

Tampa's traffic squad quota required 15 to 20 moving violation tickets per officer per day. Moving violations are tickets that add points to one's driver's license, thereby creating large, multi-year auto insurance increases. A former traffic squad sergeant provided a memo from his captain that documented this quota. A second traffic squad was added in 1999 to double traffic squad "productivity," which is the same year Florida's "extra" police pension benefits legislation was passed.

---

8  My insurance company's rates, filed with the State, revealed points on a driver's license from a single traffic ticket would increase a driver's premium by 80% to 95% for 3 years.

The patrol officer quota was explained in an e-mail, along with other quotas. It was circulated in writing about two months prior to Chief Hogue's deposition in my lawsuit. The e-mail was sent from police supervisor Jenny Terrell to Corporal Michael Baumaister, head of Tampa's "Copper Accountability Program," on August 10, 2005, and it stated the following:

> *Mike, To give a better idea of what we are needing, take a look at the attached. It illustrates what we will be using as a guide to evaluate lower producing officers. The chart, however, is designed to only reflect monthly numbers, but we will be looking at quarterly as well. We just need the numbers!*

In response, Corporal Baumaister wrote the following e-mail to Jenny Terrell on August 15, 2005.

> *RE: Officer Averages*
> *Traffic Stops: 216 yearly, 72 Quarterly, 18 Monthly*
> *Citations-Non Crash: 144 yearly, 48 quarterly, 12 monthly*
> *Street Checks: 71 yearly, 24 quarterly, 6 monthly*
> *Reports: 169 yearly, 56 quarterly, 14 monthly*
> *Arrests: 114 yearly, 38 quarterly, 10 monthly*

The e-mail communications from Terrell and Baumaister affirmed Tampa police administrators decided, in advance, how many citizens each officer must punish with tickets, arrests, and traffic stops in order to receive a good performance evaluation. The e-mail stated that quarterly quotas also will be reviewed, which were actually higher than the monthly averages. Based on the quarterly numbers, the annual average was 152 arrests, 192 tickets (non-crash), and 288 traffic stops. The e-mail was circulated to supervisors for use in performance evaluations, and a Tampa police officer gave it to me to use as evidence of quotas in my federal lawsuit.[9]

---

9   The supervisor circulated the e-mail at roll-call shortly after my federal lawsuit about Tampa's ticket quotas was reported in local newspapers. The officer who gave it to me said the supervisor did not approve of quotas.

In 2001, the Tampa Police Department transferred Officer Baumaister (the person who provided the officer averages) to help create an Analytical Crime Analysis Unit and develop a Copper (Accountability) program, consistent with Tampa's transition to a "business approach." Formalized in 2003, the unit was supervised by Corporal Baumaister, who apparently identified ticket and arrest "averages" for use in officer performance evaluations, under the pretense of "accountability." Experienced Tampa officers explained the "business approach" was advanced by giving administrative responsibilities to relatively junior officers, as they were more inclined to support policing for profit, due to their inexperience.

An example proffered was John Bennett, who later became Tampa's Assistant Police Chief. While still relatively junior, Bennett was promoted into administration, where he became an advocate for the "business approach." A sergeant disclosed Bennett spent too few years patrolling the streets, making him gullible about believing police effectiveness is best measured by an officer's ticket and arrest productivity.

Proof of both the traffic squad and patrol officer quotas also existed in each officer's annual evaluation. The evaluations specified the number of tickets, arrests, traffic stops, and reports each officer produced during the year. Each officer was rated in Traffic Law Enforcement (TLE), based on the number of moving violation (non-crash) tickets issued. Tampa officers who "Exceeded Expectations" in achieving ticket quotas were promoted, whereas officers who did not meet the quotas received a "Below Expectation" evaluation in TLE, putting them at risk for being fired.

In his deposition in my federal lawsuit, Police Chief Hogue said, *"But on the same token, it is their job to write traffic citations, enforce the traffic laws. So there's kind of a tug of war. But police officers as a general rule do not enjoy writing traffic tickets."* Consequently, officers who were unwilling to produce large numbers of tickets were not promoted. Further, they were given remediation plans and their performance was monitored quarterly in efforts to pressure them to write more traffic tickets.

The following is an example of a Tampa officer's "Below Expectation" evaluation in Traffic Law Enforcement:

*"…he wrote fifty-nine traffic crash reports during the past seven months. During that same time period, he wrote eight moving violations. With this in mind, Officer H. needs to improve in traffic law enforcement in an effort to curtail traffic crashes.*

*His Traffic Law Enforcement is his weak area. He will write non-hazardous violations, but does not spend time looking for the hazardous violations. He has been encouraged to devote time to this area. He prefers making arrests over traffic. Officer H. came up with a plan to motivate the squad in increasing arrest stats. He has a contact with corrections that gives him information on wanted subjects. This has worked favorably for him.*

*Goal #1 … needs to demonstrate an improvement in Traffic Enforcement on a daily basis.*

*He will concentrate on the hazardous moving violations that have a primary relation to increased accidents. Courtney Campbell and Memorial will be one area he targets. Also I-275 and Westshore area at the exit ramp."*

Officer H. received a "Remedial Training" plan with the expectation to write more moving violation tickets in order to *enhance the quality of life of services to citizens of Tampa*," as stated on his evaluation,[10] despite having nearly 20 years of police experience, excelling in finding persons who had warrants for their arrest, and receiving high marks for the quality of his investigations, written reports and recovering property. "Hazardous moving violations" are tickets that add points to a driver's license, thereby creating large auto insurance premium increases and "extra" police pension benefits. The zones Officer H. was told to target were speed traps, where the speed limit precipitously drops. Neither was a high crash area.

---

10 The notion that tickets and arrests improve "quality of life" for citizens is typical rhetoric among police administrators, when attempting to justify policing for profit.

Tampa police officers, then, were given an incentive to write tickets, since it could lead to promotion, as the Tampa Police Department regarded tickets as a meaningful indicator of an officer's productivity. Traffic squad officers would receive stellar performance evaluations in Traffic Law Enforcement, despite their efforts being restricted to writing moving violation tickets and recognizing they self-select for this assignment. One such traffic squad officer wrote 2,159 traffic tickets in 2002. In his glowing performance review, the supervisor wrote, "*I believe he is ready for advancement within the Department.*" The officer was reassigned to an administrative position in City Hall and promoted to Corporal—a sweet reward for his ticket productivity.

I spoke to this officer when he was on the traffic squad. He regularly monitored the school zone at a small private elementary school where the speed limit was reduced from 35 to 15 mph for 45 minutes in the morning and afternoon. In Florida, ticket fines are doubled in school zones and more driver's license points accrue, thereby creating a larger auto insurance increase. Flashing lights were not used during the reduced speed time and the signs denoting the slower times were easy to miss, as the lettering was small. The officer's car was not visible when driving through the school zone, since he hid beyond the half-block school zone. When I stopped to talk to him, he admitted most drivers he ticketed were unaware of the school zone. I suggested he park under the school zone sign with his vehicle lights flashing, thereby calling attention to the school zone and alerting drivers to slow down. He responded he would not "catch" anyone, if he followed my suggestion. By not calling attention to the school zone, elementary school children were crossing a busy street without a crossing guard, a traffic light, or flashing lights to alert drivers to the school zone. Consistent with policing for profit, the Tampa police stationed a traffic squad officer near the school zone, but *not* to assist elementary school students in crossing the street safely or to slow traffic. Instead, the officer hid to write traffic tickets to drivers who did not notice the poorly marked school zone.

Tampa's traffic squads often targeted construction zones on the local interstate, as fines and auto insurance increases (due to more driver's license points) are greater for drivers ticketed in such zones. In 2002, a local newspaper reported Tampa's traffic squad used unmarked cars, motorcycles and a helicopter to patrol the interstate. In the article, John Bennett, then a sergeant, reported the squad targets rush hour traffic. He explained the police use two unmarked SUVs to identify violators, and have nine police motorcycles stationed at entrance and exit ramps to write the tickets. A helicopter is overhead to prevent violators from getting away. Using such tactics, the squad could produce nearly 200 traffic tickets in just a few hours, consistent with traffic squad officers producing 15 to 20 moving violation tickets per officer per day. Bennett pointed out that drivers can accrue enough driver's license points in a single traffic stop to have their license revoked. He said, *"It can come out to a pretty large fine and a lot of points on your license"*—great news, if one is policing for profit. The City's website identified Tampa's top traffic crash locations, and the interstate was not listed among them, revealing the traffic squad's interstate focus was not about reducing crashes.

In 1972, the Federal Highway Administration criticized efforts, such as those used by the Tampa Police Department on the interstate, since the sole purpose is to generate revenue from poor roadway engineering.[11] A Federal Highway Administration official

---

11 In 1972, the Federal Highway Administration provided the following on the perversity of speed traps as were used in Tampa:
SELECTIVE TRAFFIC ENFORCEMENT MANUAL
January 1972
Re: FHWA Library #: TEA1400.F72
U.S. Department of Transportation
National Highway Traffic Safety Administration
Washington, D.C. 20590
DOT HS-800 701
The most visible result of quantitative, revenue-oriented, nonselective traffic law enforcement policies is the persistent use of "sitting-in" enforcement techniques. Sitting-in usually occurs at locations which, in police jargon, are referred to as "duck ponds" or "cherry patches." The sitting-in practices are particularly objectionable when two or more enforcement units group together to work an intersection, which generates frequent driver violations. Usually, where this situation occurs, the officers are doing nothing more than reaping

told me speed limits are often set lower than standards indicate (85th percentile speed) in order to write more speeding tickets. In Tampa, the interstate speed limit is 55 mph, but traffic in the left lane consistently moves at 70 mph, meaning violators are easy to find, so the Tampa police can simply choose how many tickets they want to write on any given day.

Unfortunately, ticket quotas can encourage officers who want good performance evaluations to engage in fabrications or pursue very minor infractions to meet the quota. In my federal lawsuit, as previously mentioned, I had about a dozen credible persons (neighbors, friends, co-workers, graduate students) who would testify they were victims of Tampa police ticketing fraud.[12] Also, traffic tickets can be rigged. For example, I found two people who independently report believing Tampa officers forced an alleged infraction using a decoy vehicle and then misrepresented circumstances in court. Each was following a car on a two-lane road in a no-passing zone. The forward vehicle then stopped for no apparent reason. After waiting and subsequently honking, each eventually passed the stopped vehicle (one passed on the left and the other on the right shoulder), as it is legal to pass a roadway obstruction. An officer immediately emerged, writing a ticket for illegal passing. In court, the officer denied the forward vehicle had stopped.

Tampa's third form of ticket quota was having a requirement for a ticket-at-every-crash. Florida law allows tickets to be written following a crash investigation *only* if the officer conducts a personal investigation and has probable cause that a traffic law was violated. The Tampa Police Department's written policy required neither a personal investigation nor probable cause, and instead allowed

---

the harvest of inadequate or poor traffic engineering. These locations frequently encourage noncompliance by the motorist to traffic signals or turning regulations. Very often, however, the real culprit is faulty traffic engineering, rather than the driver. Poor positioning of signals and channelization deficiencies are characteristically present at the "duck ponds."

12 Examples are provided on my website: www.highwayrobberytampa.com.

supervisors to order investigating officers to write a ticket, even if the investigating officer did not know who violated a traffic law or did not believe a traffic law was violated. Further, the City of Tampa required officers to write tickets in minor non-injury crashes that did not require a police investigation, according to Florida law. A Florida Highway Patrol captain explained to me that requiring an investigating officer to write a ticket after the officer concluded probable cause did not exist is a "color of law" crime, which is a felony.

This quota was also affirmed through officer evaluations. In officers' annual evaluations, the number of crashes investigated during the year is documented and is identical to the number of tickets issued in crash investigations, thereby revealing a ticket is issued at each crash investigation. The Tampa Police Department trained officers to believe they were paid by auto insurance companies to investigate traffic crashes and this was mandated by State law, even though it was not true (and nonsense). Tampa officers were also told in their training that in return for the insurance money, the police must write a ticket at every crash to tag a driver as *at-fault* (meaning responsible for paying damages), unrelated to whether probable cause existed to write the ticket. However, this is *not* Florida law and, in fact, who paid damages (at fault) is inadmissible in traffic ticket court hearings.

Officer Edward Bowden was the Tampa training officer who conveyed Tampa's ticket-at-every-crash policy to me, following my minor accident. He said I did not violate a traffic law, but his supervisor ordered a ticket, nonetheless, adding that my insurance company wanted a ticket issued, as well. Officer Bowden blamed the practice on the State of Florida and suggested I file a lawsuit against the State to get this remedied. This is affirmed in his deposition in my federal lawsuit. In 2005, he said the following.

*"My understanding of our procedures are, if you're actually dispatched to a crash, no matter what the involved vehicles are, you're supposed to write the report and issue the citation...The only other thing I think that I've used in any conversation is that*

*my personal perspective on some of these traffic crashes is that we're investigating them primarily for the benefit of the insurance company, that they have documentation at the time at the scene. Because as far as how it relates to police work, you know, I guess just personally, sometimes I don't see that relationship; if there's minimal damage, there's no criminal offense... If there's not a serious injury or fatality or a criminal offense, such as DUI or something else, it's the general perspective that it's for documentation for insurance."*

Thus, Officer Bowden viewed tickets issued in minor crashes as documentation for insurance and unrelated to police work. Even Tampa's Police Chief Hogue believed this practice was required, *even though it actually violated Florida law.* Chief Hogue said the following in his 2005 deposition in my federal lawsuit about why he believed the Chapter 185 revenues (from auto insurers) accrued to the police pension.

*And I had always heard prior to becoming a little more educated on it, since Ms. Orban's lawsuit, that it was for the police department investigating traffic accidents, something that the insurance companies needed the traffic accidents for whatever. And that was some sort of through the legislature had mandated that the insurance companies pay the cities for doing the traffic accidents. That's what I always thought it was. I'm not sure it's exactly that anymore. But what the funding source actually is and how it works, even to this day I don't have a clue.*

This man was the police chief of a major city, and yet remained clueless about State law regarding when officers can issue tickets in traffic crash investigations.

When probable cause did not exist to write the ticket, the crash report would "need" (in the eyes of those policing for profit) to have omissions, fabrications or both to support issuing the ticket.

Omissions occur when relevant information is not reported. Fabrications are misrepresentations of facts available to the officer, such as points of impact, weather, road conditions, or air bag deployment. Tampa's policy required officers to fabricate and/or ignore evidence when probable cause did not exist, in order to write a crash report that supported issuing the ticket.

The absurdity of ticket quotas was further revealed in Florida legislation, passed in 2004, which made Florida's Clerks of Court advocates for traffic tickets. The new law required each county's Clerk of Court to be funded from a portion of their traffic ticket revenue, thereby encouraging Florida's Clerks of Court in 67 counties to advocate for policing for profit—both tickets and convictions. In 2009, 52,000 fewer tickets were issued countywide in Hillsborough, Florida (Tampa), a one-sixth workload reduction in tickets for the Clerk (albeit *not* due to the Tampa Police Department). This necessitated downsizing the Hillsborough County Clerk of Court office from 937 to 820 employees. The Clerk of Court, Pat Frank, said, "*We are close to the edge of the cliff.*"

However, viewed differently, the Clerk of Court's revenue and staff reductions coincided with reduced tickets and workload: smaller government. Instead, the Clerk of Court wanted more tickets and revenue, and not less work. Tickets allowed her to run a larger shop—bigger government. What the Clerk of Court considered to be adverse for her was good for the public: fewer tickets to pay and a smaller Clerk of Court office to fund. Tampa residents get to keep more of their own money to spend on something other than traffic tickets and Clerk of Court staff.

While ticket and arrest quotas may be perceived as illegal, they are used by some law enforcement agencies, as evidenced by the Tampa Police Department. Federal and state laws need to explicitly ban ticket and arrest quotas, including prohibiting evaluating officers on their number of tickets or arrests. Severe sanctions should exist for law enforcement administrators who use quotas, such as decertification in law enforcement, since quotas lead to fraud. As a positive example, the Governor of Illinois signed a law in 2014 that bans local, county and state agencies from having ticket quotas, and prohibits using the number of tickets issued in officers' performance evaluations.

# CHAPTER 4

# ARREST QUOTAS

## Deciding in Advance How
## Many Citizens Must Be Jailed

*"You don't have many suspects who are innocent of a crime. If a
person is innocent of a crime, then he is not a suspect."*

Edwin Meese, 1985
U.S. Attorney General for President Reagan

A Tampa police sergeant told me achieving the arrest quota was
extremely difficult, relative to achieving the traffic ticket quota.
Toward the end of each month, she would inform her patrol squad
of the number of arrests and tickets that must be achieved by the
month's end to remain in good standing. The Tampa police tactics
used to achieve arrests were devastating for some citizens who were
falsely charged with a crime, as evidenced by the Latin Kings.

In 2006, the Tampa police and local sheriff arrested purported leaders of the Latin Kings gang, charging them with conspiracy to engage
in racketeering. The 39 arrests were first-degree felonies that carried a
maximum prison sentence of 30 years. The local sheriff, David Gee,
announced, *"This is tremendous; it's tremendous for the state of Florida."*
The sheriff's undercover deputies supposedly worked their way into the
organization in partnership with the Tampa police and FBI. The local

State Attorney, Mark Ober, advised reporters to "*stay tuned*" for more arrests. Ultimately, more than 50 people were arrested.

Then, in 2008, a judge "gutted" the case, throwing out 23 charges. It turned out the police informant was actually a felon who was paid by the Tampa police and FBI. Most of the defendants had been arrested at a mandatory meeting of the Latin Kings that was set-up by the police informant, who threatened to beat anyone (and their family) if not attending. The judge concluded many of the defendants attended only because of this threat. Evidence affirmed the Latin Kings had not been active in the Tampa area until the informant convened the meeting. It was also reported that many family members had posted bail bonds costing large sums of money for the "bogus" arrests. Other defendants had been jailed for nearly 2 years since their arrest. Others had already taken the plea deals offered.[13] In Florida, defendants who are found guilty are assessed attorney fees when represented by the public defender, which can create pressure to enter plea deals if it is a lower cost option, relative to a lengthy trial that could create significant expense.

It was further revealed that back in December 2005, the Tampa police and FBI had agreed to drop the police informant's burglary charge in return for finding drug and gun activity among the Latin Kings. At the time, the informant was in jail. Subsequently, the police provided the informant with a free apartment, a cell phone, $2,400 for monthly living expenses, and the potential for a $100,000 bonus if members of the Latin Kings were convicted. Despite the judge describing the informant as "*an out-of-control convicted felon abusing his role as an informant*," law enforcement continued to pay his monthly expenses while the State Attorney in Tampa sought a new hearing.

Defense attorneys for the Latin Kings alleged prosecutorial misconduct. After being sued, the City of Tampa police and

---

13 Some lower income defendants feel pressure to take a plea deal, agreeing to plead guilty to a lesser charge, only because they cannot afford bail and do not want to remain in jail until their trial occurs.

Hillsborough County sheriff settled with the former defendants for nearly $500,000. Despite the settlement, many former defendants reported their lives were permanently damaged by the ordeal: losing jobs, homes, and family via divorce.

The Latin Kings saga is direct and compelling evidence demonstrating why arrest quotas must be illegal. The perpetrators of the unfounded arrests were law enforcement officials who sought convictions—paying a criminal who attempted to create the appearance of crime. While more than 50 Hispanic men were set-up for the purpose of sending them to prison, consequences were absent for the law enforcement officials who orchestrated these events. Sanctions are needed to deter officials from rigging arrests to advance convictions. The Latin Kings saga also reveals the need for improved standards regarding use of police informants, as the police paid an acknowledged "out-of-control" convicted felon public monies, including offering him a bonus if convictions occurred.

With the arrests of the Latin Kings in 2006, it was the public defender who helped expose the police informant's lack of credibility. By 2014, the State Attorney was attempting to block the public defender from gaining access to backgrounds of police informants. Meanwhile, one paid Tampa police informant reported to the media he lied about a suspect to the police, which reveals standards are set very low for police informants. The public defender, as well as defense attorneys, should have access to information on police informants, as credibility concerns should clearly be considered by the court. Better laws are needed regarding police informants, as criminals are being paid to provide evidence against others—"evidence" that may or may not be true.

Further, arrest quotas can be hazardous for officers, since the opportunity to make an arrest may detract from officer safety. From 1998 to 2010, six Tampa police officers were shot and killed in the course of arresting suspects. This is a remarkably high rate—nearly 1% of Tampa's patrol force. Arrest quotas may shift priorities away from optimizing officer safety to meeting the quota.

Meanwhile, despite the arrest quota, the Tampa Police Department was underreporting the seven categories of violent and non-violent crime, in order to create the appearance to the public of greater effectiveness. The FBI's Uniform Crime Reporting System defines violent crime as: 1) murder, 2) forcible rape, 3) robbery, and 4) aggravated assault, and defines non-violent crime as: 5) burglary, 6) larceny, and 7) motor vehicle theft. These seven categories of crime are reported and compared among jurisdictions and over time.

A Tampa police sergeant clarified for me why officers believed the underreporting occurred in Tampa. In 2003, Pam Iorio was elected Tampa's mayor with a promise to reduce Tampa's high crime rates. She subsequently hired Stephen Hogue as police chief. Some officers believe she told Chief Hogue that if he did not reduce Tampa's high crime rate, she would replace him. Under Chief Hogue, the Tampa Police Department immediately changed the way some crimes were reported. For example, if an apartment building parking lot had multiple auto burglaries during a given night, the police would report it as one burglary under Chief Hogue, instead of reporting each victim as a separate auto burglary, as had been done in the past. As a consequence, auto burglaries in Tampa immediately plummeted. If this is how crime is counted, then two persons murdered in a home would count as one murder, since only one home was involved, just as only one parking lot was involved. The sergeant added that crime statistics become meaningless if counting parking lots, homes, or perpetrators, instead of each and every crime victim.

A retired Tampa police captain, Marion Lewis, said the following about the Tampa Police Department's (TPD) changes in reporting crime: "*Crime stats are reported on the honor code, and TPD is being dishonorable.*" He went on to contend the police department was underreporting crime to create crime statistics that suggest improvement. He even contended one particular murder had not been reported as a murder.

As John Bennett expressed in his deposition in my federal lawsuit, the Tampa police used a crime reporting method similar to

CompStat, which was used by the New York City Police Department (NYPD). CompStat is a management approach to reduce crime by geographically mapping crime, identifying problems, and holding supervisors accountable for reducing crime. It is coupled with "zero tolerance" for petty crime, which increases the number of arrests and helps to achieve any arrest quota, such as existed in Tampa. Comp-Stat was launched in 2000 by Mayor Rudolph Giuliani and Police Commissioner Bernard Kerik as a "*quality of life initiative*" to target infractions related to noise, squeegees, graffiti, panhandling, public consumption of alcohol, prostitution, and homelessness. *The New York Times* reported the CompStat philosophy assumes "*aggressive enforcement against minor quality of life crimes, like loitering and fare-beating, deters further petty crime and ultimately drives down major crime.*" Thus, one CompStat assumption is that targeting minor offenses will reduce major crime.

However, targeting minor offenses is, by definition, policing for profit and the opposite of community policing. Tampa officers construed it differently, saying that with community policing, officers used minor offenses to educate the public, in contrast to an opportunity for an arrest. For example, if a youth was engaged in underage drinking in a public place, a Tampa officer told me he would make the young person pour the beverage out and put the container in a trash can. The officer would then tell the youth if he or she was found doing this again, the person would be arrested. Then, the officer would discuss the consequences and costs of an arrest. Thus, officers gave people, especially younger and low-income persons, a break over minor offenses, while also attempting to educate them about the potential consequences of their behavior.

Further, Tampa officers who embraced community policing (as opposed to the business approach) advocated for a written warning system to track minor violations, including traffic violations, to avoid writing tickets or making arrests for minor offenses, which would also allow for identifying persons who have prior warnings. The community policing philosophy is particularly important, since the reasoning-rational thinking part of the brain does not fully develop until 25 years of age, meaning younger persons are more likely to demonstrate poor judgment. Community policing is oriented toward helping people to abide by the law, especially young persons, whereas the business approach focuses on maximizing tickets, arrests, property seizures, convictions, and ultimately, revenue.

In 2010, John Eterno (retired NYPD captain) and Eli Silverman (professor emeritus of criminal justice) released their survey results of former NYPD police officials regarding CompStat. The findings were critical of how the NYPD compiled crime statistics, in particular their downgrading serious crimes to less serious offenses. The report concluded, *"A close review of the NYPD's statistics and analysis demonstrate that the misclassification of reports may have an appreciable effect on certain reported crime rates."* The New York Times reported this survey of more than 100 high-ranking retired NYPD officials found officers *"were aware over the years of instances of 'ethically inappropriate' changes to complaints of crimes in the seven categories measured by the department's signature CompStat program."*

While crime in New York City was being annually reported as reduced, questions have emerged about whether the statistics were accurate. For example, officers had ways to lower estimated values of stolen property that resulted in reporting a misdemeanor, rather than a felony. Further, some crime victims were persuaded not to report their crime. John Eterno and Eli Silverman wrote a book detailing abuses, titled, *The Crime Numbers Game: Management by Manipulation (Advances in Police Theory and Practice).* The NYPD eventually conducted its own analysis in 2011 and concluded data manipulation had occurred regarding crime statistics.

While CompStat's geographic mapping of crime to identify problems is sound, the effort should be expected to fail if not educating supervisors on effective strategies to use, once having the crime mapping information. Simply informing supervisors that crime numbers must be reduced, absent specific strategies to use, can be expected to result in underreporting of crime, since supervisors will maneuver to achieve the crime reductions needed to get a good performance evaluation, just as officers maneuver to achieve any ticket or arrest quota.

Oddly, NYPD Police Commissioner Bernard Kerik, who helped launch CompStat, later pled guilty to eight felonies. His CompStat system did not deter him from becoming a criminal. He had accepted $280,000 in apartment renovations from a construction company seeking government contracts and lied to the White House when considered for the position of Secretary for the Department of Homeland Security. In 2010, he pled guilty to charges of tax fraud, criminal conspiracy and lying under oath. He was sentenced to four years in prison. In an interview after his release from prison, he was critical of the harshness with which he was treated by the justice system. Apparently, he no longer embraced the "zero tolerance" philosophy that he once advanced as police commissioner.

The NYPD supposedly underreported the seven categories of violent and non-violent crime. Instead, arresting people for loitering, fare beating, trespassing, drug possession, racketeering, prostitution, etc. did not add to violent or non-violent crime statistics. Consequently, if wanting to appear effective in lowering crime among the seven categories of crime, while also having (and "pushing" officers to meet) arrest quotas, a deterrent exists to report violent and non-violent crimes, while encouraging arrests for minor or petty infractions.

In Tampa, I learned how the police could avoid reporting a crime for the purpose of improving Tampa's crime statistics, since it happened to me. In 2007, the owner of a check cashing shop called me, because he believed a man was attempting to cash a $400 forged check from my account. After finding it was one of three checks missing from the back of my checkbook, I went to the shop where the accused man was now sitting in the back of a sheriff deputy's patrol car. I did not know the man and had not written the check to him, so deputies arrested him and he was prosecuted. It was easy to determine how he got the check, since he was accompanied by a new maid from the service we used. Deputies did not arrest her, because she denied knowing me.

One sheriff's deputy instructed me to report the three stolen checks, as well as the maid, to the Tampa police, since the theft occurred in the City of Tampa limits. A Tampa police patrol officer promptly arrived and wrote a police report. Then, my case was assigned to Det. Davis who called a few days later. I told him the same man had cashed one of the other two checks for $240 prior to his arrest, and a credit card was missing and used for nearly $1,000 in purchases. The credit card company had contacted me about the fraudulent activity. In addition, I informed the detective that jewelry and an iPod worth about $500 were missing, but later discovered more missing jewelry, making the loss about $1,000. Det. Davis told me to mail the credit card and check information to him, but indicated he did not plan to take action. By not reporting the additional losses, the detective avoided reporting or making an arrest for a larceny, which is the crime associated with the stolen iPod and jewelry, thereby reducing Tampa's non-violent crime statistics.

I then called the sheriff's deputy, who said he could not intervene since the theft occurred in Tampa. The deputy explained it was an easy crime to solve. The man was still in jail, meaning the Tampa police had ready access to charge him over the $240 forged check he had cashed. The deputy said the Tampa detective should go to the WalMart where the credit card was used and watch the surveillance video to view who had used the card. He also said sheriff deputies had already notified the Tampa Police Department of the pawn shop where the maid had pawned items stolen from another house, for which they arrested her. They had informed the Tampa Police Department the maid had pawned jewelry in the evening after she'd last worked at my house. He said Det. Davis should take a description of my missing property, go to the pawn shop, and see if it was pawned there by the maid.

I called Det. Davis and explained what the deputy said he should do. Davis responded by saying he planned to do nothing, which is what he did. He never wrote a police report about the cashed forged check, credit card purchases, or missing property. He never went to the jail to charge the man over the cashed forged check. He did not watch the surveillance video or visit the pawn shop. He let the maid and her accomplice keep everything: $240 in cash, nearly $1,000 in credit card purchases, and about $1,000 in jewelry and an iPod. Det. Davis completed the patrol officer's report about the three missing checks by stating he called the maid, she did not call him back, so he closed the case.[14]

I had difficulty getting the credit card purchases written off, since the credit card company wanted a police report number. For months, they sent bills with late fees and interest assessed. I left messages for Det. Davis, informing him the credit card company needed a police report to write off the charges; but he never responded. Eventually, someone from the credit card company called me and said it was time to provide a police report number or pay the bill. Instead, I gave him the contact information of retired Tampa police captain Marion Lewis. Newspapers had reported former Captain Lewis's contention that the Tampa police do not report certain crimes, in order to create the appearance of a lower crime rate. After reading his allegation in the news, I had called him and he told me the Tampa police did not report the theft at my house in order to achieve one less crime in their statistics, consistent with his criticisms of the Tampa Police Department. I asked my credit card company to call the retired police captain, as he could explain why a police report was not written. The $1,000 in credit card charges, interest and late fees were subsequently written off—all thanks to retired Captain Lewis (no thanks to the Tampa Police Department).

Some months later, local newspapers reported the Tampa police had further lowered crime. I contacted my City Councilman, explained my experience, and contended crime was being

---

14  Det. Davis concludes the police report as follows:
   "*It seems that Ms. Hernandez was arrested for her involvement in the theft of jewelry while working for the maid service. I was able to obtain some pertinent information so that I might arrange an interview with the suspect. After making several attempts to contact the suspect the case will be closed due to lack of evidence. If at anytime I should make contact with the suspect, the case will be reopened at that time.*"

underreported. The Councilman demanded an explanation from the Tampa Police Department. The police assigned a new detective to my case, who admitted Det. Davis failed to report or investigate the crime. The new detective said it was now too late to do so.

One has to wonder, what *were* Tampa's real crime statistics? Meanwhile, Tampa's Mayor, Pam Iorio, gave some police administrators bonuses for reducing Tampa's crime rate, apparently never paying attention to how they did so.

Similar to ticket and arrest quotas, Tampa's "traffic stop" quota can also create pressure on officers to act absent probable cause. Traffic stops generate revenue, because they provide opportunities to identify persons with warrants for their arrest or who are in possession of illegal drugs, which helps to achieve the arrest quota, while also increasing "profit" from impounding or seizing the vehicle. Impound fees are an additional revenue generator and are charged per day, even if a conviction does not occur.

For example, I worked with someone who was arrested for DUI after a Tampa traffic squad officer followed him out of the parking lot at a bar. The officer alleged the stop was due to a broken taillight, but a taillight was not actually broken. Then, the officer said he smelled alcohol on the driver's breath. The driver believed he passed the field sobriety test, so he refused the breath test, believing the officer lacked probable cause to request it. The driver knew that in Florida, a DUI arrest can be made with a blood alcohol level less than .08 if the officer believes the driver is impaired, which is a subjective conclusion in a police department that uses arrest quotas. The driver opted to have a jury decide whether or not he appeared impaired. The man was not convicted of DUI, but nonetheless he lost his impounded truck. The impound fees were around $1,000, which he could not afford, since he had to hire an attorney over the DUI arrest. Thus, arrests from traffic stops provide another revenue stream for the police, since they either collect impound fees or take possession of the vehicle, regardless of whether a conviction occurs.

Further, if a traffic stop results in a driver's arrest for drug dealing, the vehicle and cash are seized, becoming the property of the police. Current laws regarding such seizures are designed to make it difficult for owners to regain possession of their property. In 2015, a Florida legislator sponsored a bill whereby seized property would be given to charity to deter police from using property seizures to generate funds for themselves. A Florida sheriff explained his opposition to the bill, contending seized property is needed to buy equipment for law enforcement agencies, since their budgets are tight. In contrast, law enforcement agencies could opt to manage on the budgets provided to them, for example, by purchasing less equipment.

When law enforcement agencies use arrest quotas, their typical focus is on arrests *other* than the seven categories of crime that comprise violent and non-violent crime statistics, in order to create the appearance of effectiveness. Consequently, arrest quotas target other crimes or infractions, particularly minor offenses that allow for revenue generation and property seizures. For this reason, FBI and state crime statistics should report arrests and convictions for *all* types of offenses, including local ordinances, and not just the seven "main" categories, in order to identify jurisdictions that have excessive arrest rates, especially over minor offenses. In addition, the race/ethnicity distribution should be provided for each type of arrest to assess whether discrimination is occurring.

For example, in 2015, the *Tampa Bay Times* reported the Tampa police wrote disproportionately higher numbers of tickets to bicyclists relative to other Florida cities, and that 80% were written to black bicyclists. Racial profiling could well be reduced if the demographic mix of a jurisdiction's arrests and tickets, by type of infraction, is readily accessible public information.

## CHAPTER 5

# HOME RULE

## An Excuse for Public Officials
## To Twist the Law

*"Orban's further allegation of constitutional injury resulting from the City's "policy" of allowing officers to submit "crash reports" is equally moot and otherwise without merit. The Senior Administrative Judge for the Traffic Division for the City specifically allows officers of the police department to submit reports in place of live testimony."*

Federal District Steven D. Merryday
from *Orban v. City of Tampa*

"Home rule" allows municipalities to establish local rules (ordinances) to conduct business "except as otherwise provided by law."[15] This means local rules can be used, but they must conform with existing laws. Home rule does not allow for violating state or federal laws, but this is not how the Tampa Police Department, local court, or federal Judge Steven Merryday interpreted "home rule."

---

15 Article VIII, Section 2(b) of the Florida Constitution:
  *"Municipalities shall have governmental, corporate and proprietary powers to enable them to conduct municipal government, perform municipal functions and render municipal services, and may exercise power for municipal purposes except as otherwise provided by law."*

Delving into Tampa's ticket-at-every-crash policy revealed a sinister dimension. Under the pretense of home rule, the local court allowed crash reports to be used as evidence, even though Florida law bans their use in court, because they are hearsay. Further, crash reports were used as "secret" (*ex parte*) evidence for the judge's perusal only, and never entered into the court record, so drivers would not know the report existed, much less that the report was being used as evidence. Local judges who used the reports in this manner were violating Florida law.[16] Also, in Tampa, any police officer who wrote a ticket and crash report was not required to attend the traffic ticket hearing, despite being subpoenaed to court. This means the police evidence against a driver was the secret crash report, which federal Judge Merryday ultimately fully endorsed, even though submitted as secret hearsay evidence *in violation of Florida law.*

Judge Merryday's quotation that begins this chapter, from his ruling in my federal court case, correctly reports the practice of submitting crash reports as evidence began when local Traffic Division Judge Thomas Stringer sent a memo on March 29, 1985 to local law enforcement agencies and the State Attorney. However, Judge Merryday ignored the fact that Florida law bans the use of such reports in court. Judge Stringer's memo stated officers can send the crash report in lieu of the officer appearing in person on traffic tickets written in crash investigations, provided the officer did not witness anything relevant.[17]

---

16 Florida Statute 316.066 states the following: "...each crash report made by a person involved in a crash and any statement made by such person to a law enforcement officer for the purpose of completing a crash report required by this section shall be without prejudice to the individual so reporting. Such report or statement may not be used as evidence in any trial, civil or criminal."

17 Judge Stringer wrote the following in his memo. "Also effectively [sic] immediately, officers who issue a citation in an accident case where the officer did not witness the accident may continue to file their accident reports in lieu of their appearance in court, *provided* there is nothing that the officer witnessed that would be relevant; and further provided that the officer has listed the appropriate witnesses on a witness list."

The point is, Judge Merryday was incorrect in his quotation above in assuming this practice was legal, since it violated State law and likely federal laws. Tampa's police attorney *clearly* understood the practice was illegal, but permitted it nonetheless. Prior to my lawsuit, my attorney wrote a letter to the City of Tampa attorney requesting corrections to the false entries on my crash report and providing the supporting documentation, since my auto insurance company offered to refund a nearly $4,000 premium surcharge, if the Tampa police corrected the report. In response, Tampa police attorney, Kirby Rainsberger, refused to make the changes, despite admitting the report had errors. He further wrote that crash reports are inadmissible to court, writing: "*Fortunately, all of the foregoing is unnecessary because what the drivers involved in the accident tell the investigating officer is privileged and inadmissible in any court pursuant to Florida Statute 316.066 (subject to qualifications not applicable in this case).*" Thus, Tampa's police attorney knew crash reports were inadmissible in court. Nonetheless, the Tampa Police Department's written policy permitted their submission to court, as stated in their Traffic Citations policy.[18] Judge Merryday ignored Florida law in his ruling, as well as the use of these reports as secret evidence.

The submission of crash reports as *ex parte* evidence also appears to violate federal laws. A U.S. Supreme Court ruling regarding witness testimony is provided below.

*Under Crawford, a witness's testimony against a defendant is inadmissible unless the witness appears at trial or, if the witness*

---

18 Tampa Police Policy—634 Traffic Citations—states the following about subpoenas issued in a traffic crash (page 4): "*If so, the officer will not have to appear in court through an agreement with traffic judges. In order to be relieved of the responsibility of appearing in court, officers must obtain a copy of the crash report and a pre-printed memo available in the District Administrative CSO's offices. The memo must be completed, attached to the report copy and subpoena and submitted to the officer's supervisor.*" This information is then provided to administration, which "*will deliver them to the deputy clerk of violations who will place them in the applicable court file.*"

*is unavailable, the defendant had a prior opportunity for cross examination. 541 U. S., at 54.*

The officer is the witness who observes circumstances following an accident and questions the drivers. Per Florida law, the officer also decides whether (or not) to write a ticket based on the evidence, which requires probable cause to issue a ticket. The officer then serves as the prosecutor in traffic court, if a ticket is written. However, in Tampa, officers do not attend hearings on tickets issued in crash investigations, which precludes any cross-examination about their rationale for the ticket or crash report entries. Because the reports are not entered into the record as evidence, the officer's crash report testimony is unknown to the defendant, making it impossible to refute. The judge can then declare a driver's statements are not supported by the police, even though a police officer is not in attendance. I know this, because it happened to me. Drivers are disadvantaged, since they are not provided with the report, much less able to query the officer who wrote the ticket and report. Nonetheless, federal district judge Steven Merryday had no concerns about the practice of submitting false crash reports as secret evidence to court hearings because a local traffic judge, Thomas Stringer, approved the practice.

Similar to former NYPD police commissioner Bernard Kerik, Judge Thomas Stringer was also charged with a felony—bank fraud. The judge admitted to lying on a loan application when purchasing a house in Hawaii using a stripper's money as the down payment. He was subsequently disbarred after accepting a plea deal.

Meanwhile, in Tampa, drivers in minor crashes were tricked into believing they had the crash report, since the officer provides a 1-page "short form crash report" (i.e., "exchange of information") at the scene, which includes information about the drivers, vehicles, and insurance companies. Consequently, drivers would not expect a second 4-page "long form crash report" to exist, which provides the accident circumstances that justify issuing the ticket. The "short form crash report" is the correct form to use in minor non-injury crashes, as the long form report is for injury crashes and those involving a crime, e.g., DUI. Nonetheless, in minor non-injury crashes, the Tampa police required officers to complete a 4-page "long form crash report" for the purpose of submitting it as secret evidence to the traffic ticket hearing, as well as filing it with the State for use by auto insurance companies to increase driver's premiums, which created a nearly $4,000 insurance increase for me.

The secret submission of crash reports to traffic hearings in Tampa is an example of the police, Clerk of Court and local judges colluding to violate Florida laws for the purpose of advancing convictions, thereby increasing revenue for the police and court, as well as creating large auto insurance increases. Their excuse for deviating from State law was "home rule." However, public officials in Tampa ignored the exception ("as otherwise provided by law"). Florida law bans the use of crash reports in court, as Tampa police attorney Rainsberger had explained. In my lawsuit, even federal district Judge Steven Merryday played along and sanctioned this Tampa police policy, pretending county Judge Stringer could approve this practice, despite it clearly violating State law and likely federal court rulings. Despite being a federal judge, Judge Merryday was just another member of Tampa's "good old boy" court and conviction network, pretending as if a local traffic judge had the authority to inform law enforcement agencies and the State Attorney that they need not abide by State law.

Although Judge Stringer had approved this local practice, the Tampa Police Department could have required officers to abide by State law and attend court hearings. Judge Stringer made the submission of crash reports optional, and not mandatory. Instead, Tampa's policy allowed for submitting crash reports to court, in lieu of the officer attending, in direct violation of Florida law.

A young Tampa patrol officer told me he hoped I could get this policy changed. He said it was disconcerting to write a ticket per a supervisor's order, especially when not knowing who caused the crash. He said he investigated an un-witnessed red-light running injury crash. Both drivers claimed to have a green light and he did not know who was telling the truth. His supervisor told him to choose either driver and write a ticket, which the officer said was troubling, since he randomly selected one driver as causing the major crash with injuries. Another Tampa officer said he investigated a red-light running crash and ticketed both drivers, because he did not know who had run the red light. The officer said he documented two diagrams on the crash report, with one each showing a different driver running the red light. Obviously, he did not have probable cause to write two tickets, much less one.

As another example of using "home rule" while violating State law, some Florida jurisdictions passed local ordinances to permit red-light camera ticket programs at the time such programs were illegal in Florida. These jurisdictions ignored the Florida Attorney General's written opinion that explained such programs were not legal, yet these jurisdictions used "home rule" as a excuse to nonetheless use the revenue-generating cameras by passing a local ordinance. Many of these jurisdictions were sued over their illegal camera programs and lost. However, the lawsuits did not result in any consequences for the public officials who approved the camera programs at the time they were illegal. Consequently, "home rule" becomes a reason for public officials to violate laws, since oversight and sanctions do not currently exist when jurisdictions enact policies or ordinances that violate laws, at least not in Florida.

Around 2001, I began advising the Florida Attorney General's Division of Economic Crimes in their investigation of some health insurance plans, which were denying benefits to beneficiaries. I asked them why local governments can violate State laws without any consequences. The answer was that laws make certain practices illegal, but the legislature does not establish a means of enforcement, meaning abiding by the law is often voluntary for public officials— an honor system. Clearly, this honor system is not working.

Meanwhile, Tampa provides many examples of how local ordinances are used to advance policing for profit, each designed to create a wealth transfer from the public to the police and court.

In 1999 (the onset of policing for profit in Tampa), Tampa City Councilman Bob Buckhorn advanced a local ordinance on behalf of the police that they might further profit from vehicles impounded by the police. The ordinance allowed the police to seize a driver's vehicle when making certain arrests, such as soliciting a prostitute or buying drugs, which allowed the police to assess an additional $850 fee to regain possession of the car (in addition to usual towing and impound fees). Drivers could request a hearing with a hearing officer hired by the City of Tampa, but the ordinance stipulated, "*The formal rules of evidence will not apply at the final hearing and hearsay evidence is admissible,*" meaning, don't expect to win. Absent payment of the fee, the Tampa police could sell the vehicle. The ordinance disappeared after challenged on legal grounds, as the State already had penalties for persons convicted of crimes, such as soliciting prostitutes or buying drugs.

Once elected as Tampa's mayor in 2011, Bob Buckhorn again advanced an ordinance that allowed seizing vehicles in arrests for soliciting a prostitute or buying drugs, with a $500 fee to recoup the vehicle (in addition to the usual towing and impound fees). A City Councilwoman opposed the ordinance, stating the fee is assessed even when defendants are found "not guilty."

As mayor, Bob Buckhorn selected a seized SUV, which had been used in sex trafficking, as his personal family car. The practice of using seized vehicles as personal property among Tampa police administrators had started long before Mayor Buckhorn's participation. In 2010, a year before Buckhorn was elected mayor, this Tampa Police Department tradition was criticized by the Institute for Justice in their policing for profit report on civil asset forfeiture. Nonetheless, Tampa's local rules increased the likelihood of seized vehicles becoming police property, while also allowing public officials to personally enjoy vehicles they seized.

Home rule can also be used to increase the number of arrests, making it easier for officers to achieve arrest quotas. "New rules" (home rules) can identify additional behaviors over which officers can make an arrest, thereby increasing the number of arrests—good news for officers struggling to meet the arrest quota. For example, in 1999, City Councilman Bob Buckhorn advanced an ordinance that required strippers to remain six feet from clients when performing "lap dances." The ordinance could result in strip club owners being sentenced to a maximum of six months in jail. Although the stated purpose was to deter the transmission of sexually transmitted diseases (STDs), the local health department director explained to the City Council that naked strippers cannot transmit STDs to clothed clients. Nonetheless, the ordinance passed and some Tampa police officers were paid to engage in "stripper surveillance": watching and arresting strippers. This ordinance also faced court challenges, due to the lack of rationale for the 6-foot limit.

Meanwhile, Councilman Buckhorn was responsible for yet another policing for profit initiative. In 2002, he advanced an ordinance that would allow people to be arrested if engaging in activities such as "flagging down people, exchanging packages on the street, or getting in and out of cars on the same block," which reduced the threshold for making an arrest in certain high crime areas of Tampa. While such behavior is not illegal, the Councilman sought to give the police authority to arrest such persons, but only in areas specified as High Intensity Drug Areas. This appeared, though, to be discrimination, since people living outside of these areas can engage in the same behaviors and not risk arrest.

As mayor, Bob Buckhorn advanced a red-light camera ordinance, since such programs had by then become legal in Florida. At the time, scientific research had concluded red-light cameras are associated with significant increases in crashes and injuries, indicating his program was about money and not safety. Mayor Buckhorn's red-light program used minimum yellow light timings, in order to maximize the number of tickets issued—nearly 70,000 tickets in the first year. However, the profitability of Tampa's camera program plummeted once the State mandated longer yellow light timings. In 2015, a news reporter disclosed Mayor Buckhorn had accepted a $10,000 contribution to his political action committee from Tampa's red-light camera vendor, American Traffic Solutions, and one of his top political advisors receives funding from this same camera vendor. As mayor, Buckhorn failed to disclose the change in rear-end crashes at camera sites by only reporting crashes that occurred within 25 feet from the intersection, whereas credible studies use 100 to 150 feet.

When the Republican National Convention came to Tampa in 2012, Mayor Buckhorn used part of the $50 million in federal funds to create a "military state" in the downtown area, using some funds to purchase an armored truck, excessive surveillance cameras that were retained after the convention, SWAT team equipment (helmets, face shields and body armor), and fences to contain the public. Mayor Buckhorn defended his "wall of law enforcement" on the pretense of public safety.

Local officials emptied a jail in anticipation of the large number of arrests they would make. However, few citizens attended the RNC activities downtown after the Tampa police announced their plans for an "arrest-fest." The City Attorney said, "*We're a little baffled. I'm not sure if it means that people don't want to go where we want them to go, or if they're just not coming.*" They weren't coming.

The National Lawyers Guild later released a report that chronicled what occurred: "*The sheer number of police, weaponry and the constant threat of aggression and arrest had a chilling effect on free speech and assembly, which led to smaller and less robust demonstrations than those in previous years.*" In contrast, Charlotte, North Carolina held the Democratic National Convention, similarly receiving $50 million in federal funds. Instead of a military state, they had a street festival for the public.

Tampa provides an excellent example of how "home rule" is used to pass local ordinances that advance policing for profit, creating more and more opportunities for the Tampa Police Department to ticket, arrest, fine, and seize property from local residents, as well as achieve convictions from crash reports that are used as secret evidence, which federal Judge Steven Merryday ultimately sanctioned (albeit the federal appellate court made his ruling disappear).

# CHAPTER 6

# KANGAROO COURTS

## Where Everyone Is Guilty, But Given Their Day in Court

*"By policy, the training officer was correct as TPD does have a policy to attempt to identify the at-fault party, and cite accordingly...You received a citation for being at-fault in a traffic crash, where the senior officer was attempting to minimize the experience with your insurance company. Unfortunately, it never made it to fruition."*

Letter to me from Sgt. John Bennett,
Executive Officer to Tampa Police Chief Bennie Holder
September 11, 2000

It is pointless for law enforcement agencies to generate excessive numbers of tickets and arrests if a majority will be dismissed in court. Consequently, judges and prosecutors are needed to act as "business partners" for successful policing for profit, which requires disingenuous court proceedings.

A "kangaroo court" is one in which the outcome is determined in advance, with the hearing merely acting out the steps of a court process. Such sham legal proceedings are *not* impartial and always to the detriment of the accused. Kangaroo court justice is one that denies due process rights, such as the right to summon witnesses or enter evidence (or by allowing the *secret* submission of false crash reports for the judge's perusal only). The court system can financially advantage itself by operating kangaroo courts.

In 2006, *The New York Times* reported its investigation into the State of New York's "justice courts" in towns and villages. While the majority of court business was traffic tickets, the justices also presided over small claim cases and preliminary hearings in felony cases. The investigation found nearly three-fourths of the part-time justices were not lawyers. Instead, they held other occupations such as truck driver, boat hauler, sewer worker, as well as former police officer. Lawyers reported to perceive many as incompetent. Some had only a high school diploma, whereas others did not even complete high school. One justice said, "*I just follow my own common sense, and the hell with the law.*" Another said, "*You've got to use your own judgment. That's why they call us judges. The law is not always right.*" To serve as a justice in New York, an individual without a law degree must complete a 6-day course provided by the state and pass a true-false test, getting at least 70% of the 50 questions correct. An example of a true-false question was provided: "Town and village justices must maintain dignity, order and decorum in their courtrooms." The news article reported "*overwhelming evidence that decade after decade and up to this day, people have often been denied fundamental legal rights.*"

Local courts can consolidate power in the hands of persons who are unqualified or ill-suited for the job, such as former police officers or sewer workers. One rationale that supports employing non-expert personnel is revealed in a statement made by Edwin Meese (U.S. Attorney General for President Reagan) in 1985: "*You don't have many suspects who are innocent of a crime... If a person is innocent of a crime, then he is not a suspect.*" If believing this is true, then the need for an impartial hearing is negated.

This notion is further bolstered by a belief that if the suspect did not commit the offense as charged, they did something equally as bad, so it really doesn't matter if the correct charge is used. This was evidenced by comments made by a former Pinellas County (Florida) sheriff. A newspaper reported his deputies arrested a woman for drug dealing. She was jailed for 81 days, unable to afford bail while awaiting trial. Prosecutors eventually concluded the wrong person was arrested, as she did not fit the description of the wanted suspect. The County offered her $8,100 ($100 per day) for the wrongful arrest, which the woman rejected as insulting. The sheriff responded, "*She's not going to be traumatized by being in jail. She probably thought she was guilty.*" There may be an underlying belief in the minds of those who promote policing for profit: the public is strewn with criminals, and if someone did not commit a crime as charged, they very likely did something equally as bad. Hence, any mistakes on the part of law enforcement ought to be viewed in the light of the old saying, "They had it coming."

As an example of kangaroo court, in a sworn statement, a Tampa traffic magistrate explained why he *always* believes the police officer in traffic ticket hearings. The statement was taken in a 2001 Internal Affairs investigation of a Tampa police sergeant who told a driver the speeding ticket he received was *not* credible. The ticket was written by the squad's corporal, who reported to the sergeant. The ticket had been written for "Speed Too Fast for Conditions," and the sergeant explained there were no prevailing conditions that would necessitate a lower speed, such as rain or fog. Nonetheless, the Tampa Police Department's IAB investigated the sergeant for aiding the ticketed driver. In a sworn statement from the investigation, the magistrate said he did not allow the driver to provide the sergeant's information in court. When the ticketed driver started to convey the sergeant's rationale, the magistrate said he "*immediately cut him off*" and found him guilty, a decision that had nothing to do with whether or not the man was driving too fast for road conditions.[19] The sergeant was

---

19 The magistrate judge stated his perspective as follows:

"*He disputed what the officer had testified to and then said that he had talked to the officer's sergeant, who told him to come to court and how to beat the case. At that point, I entered a guilty finding and dismissed the presence from me immediately. Because it was obvious that he was guilty.... You're supposed to be neutral, but you become then, to form an opinion as to the honor of the individuals involved; and I have never had a reason to doubt that officer at all in my courtroom, as far as his honor is concerned.*"

ultimately cleared of wrongdoing, because his information did not affect the verdict. The driver was found guilty.

From the court's perspective, the best strategy when policing for profit is to hire traffic magistrates who find *everyone* guilty.[20] When my federal lawsuit was reported in newspapers around 2005, a former local Tampa traffic magistrate contacted my attorney. She called him to convey her concerns that she believed the court terminated her employment because she did not find enough drivers guilty.

I experienced kangaroo court twice in Tampa, but ultimately got both tickets dismissed by proving the officer was untruthful. In 1999, the advent of Tampa's policing for profit, my neighbor received a ticket from an officer for failure to stop at a stop sign in our neighborhood, despite his claiming to have stopped. Then, the same thing happened to me *with the same officer at the same intersection.* The officer told me his radar reported that I rolled the stop sign at 7 miles per hour (mph). I had come to a full stop at the intersection and asked him to explain what he observed regarding my car. He said he was not watching my car, but was fixated on his radar. This explained why he was incorrect.

Radar takes measurements at points in time, such that he could not know my lowest speed simply by having a radar reading. However, I subsequently learned from Tampa officers that their radar could *not* measure stopping or low rates of speed, such as 7 mph. They also said their radar could only be used with the officer standing in front of or behind a moving vehicle, whereas the policeman who wrote my ticket had been perpendicular to my line of travel.

At the final traffic court hearing, the room was packed with ticketed drivers. Officers sat in a separate area near the magistrate, jostling about with elbowing, smirking, back-slapping, like a bunch of fraternity brothers. Most officers were young, white men. Ticketed drivers were diverse: black, white, Hispanic, Asian, young and old, men and women.

---

20 In Florida, traffic magistrates are appointed by the local court's Chief Judge.

The traffic magistrate began proceedings for all cases scheduled at the 6:00 p.m. hour. He was a former Tampa police officer who subsequently became a lawyer. The magistrate began by calling roll, requiring each ticket recipient to stand. He would suspend the driver's license of those failing to be present, even if the driver arrived minutes later. In contrast, judges do not call roll and instead take each case one at a time. This means, if arriving a few minutes late, one would only have their license suspended if being the first case heard during the hour. Judges are elected and thus more accountable to the community, unlike traffic magistrates who are appointed by the Chief Judge of the local court.

After roll call, the magistrate announced the names of "lucky" ticket recipients. The officers who wrote their citations were absent and their tickets were dismissed. However, this practice was later abandoned as policing for profit became more aggressive. Instead of dismissing such tickets, another final hearing date was scheduled.

The magistrate proceeded to take each case in alphabetic order, one by one, finding each driver guilty, then assessing fines, court costs, and driver's license points. When officers and drivers disagreed on circumstances, the magistrate consistently sided with the officer, even for infractions that seemed trivial. Most penalties were $90, if paid without a court hearing, but court costs added further expense; so requesting a hearing increased what drivers would pay upon conviction, along with the points on their driver's license that would create significant auto insurance increases.

An elderly woman explained her ticket was issued while her husband was in the hospital and he died shortly thereafter. The ticket was for some minor infraction. The elderly woman stood in front of the crowded court room and publicly declared being officially certified as too poor to pay the ticket. She presented the magistrate with a "Certificate of Indigence" and proof of her husband's hospitalization and death. Nonetheless, the magistrate announced fines and court costs totaling around $200. The woman wept, reporting she had no money to pay. It was like something from a Dickens novel. While she cried, the magistrate announced the elderly woman would pay the penalty by providing 40 hours of community service.

The magistrate then called me forward, along with Officer M. My husband and 11-year old daughter came forward, as well. Officer M. touted writing 6,000 citations in his 14 years of Tampa police experience. The officer reported running radar to measure my speed at the stop sign as 7 mph, which was not possible to do. He also reported using radar perpendicular to my line of travel, an angle that was not credible. My husband and I explained that the Tampa police radar could not be used in the manner described by the officer. The magistrate responded that he did not have a problem with the officer's radar use because he was presiding over his own version of kangaroo court.

He then asked my 11-year old daughter about the circumstances, as she had been in the car when I got the ticket. She told him the officer said he used radar. The magistrate asked her if I had stopped. She responded, "I don't know." He repeated his question, asking her if I stopped, and she again responded she didn't know. Although he had asked his question and it had been answered, he continued to ask the same question, raising his voice. My daughter began shaking and started to cry. He was intimidating her. I tried to intervene, but he silenced me. My daughter eventually said that perhaps I was maybe going "really slow." The magistrate declared the State had proved its case! In reality, the magistrate intimidated a child until getting the response he sought, which is not proving a case.

The magistrate opened my driving record and fumbled about, as he learned I did not have any tickets. He then withheld adjudication and assessed $47 in court costs; no fine or driver's license points. The Tampa Police Department would receive nothing, but the court still profited from hiring the unfair magistrate. As I departed, Officer M. asked to have his two other cases heard, which were tickets written at the same intersection with the same failure to stop charge.

The next day, I called Officer M.'s squad sergeant, Sgt. Stephens, and described how Officer M. claimed to use radar. Sgt. Stephens pointed out a bigger problem; Officer M. was not certified to use radar. Sgt. Stephens said he would review the hearing transcript. The sergeant subsequently contended Officer M. never mentioned radar in court and suggested my husband and I were lying. I purchased the court transcript from the Clerk of Court. Once having the transcript, I called Sgt. Stephens and read the section where the officer discussed his radar use. The sergeant sent the squad's corporal to my house.

Corporal Niemi arrived and seemed nervous. He had been assigned to listen to the recording, but admitted he could not understand what was being said. The corporal confided that Officer M. wrote the ticket because the City of Tampa gives the police department *"revenue targets"* to achieve. Officer M. was working in my neighborhood to achieve the City's revenue targets.

Sgt. Stephens then referred the matter to their Internal Affairs Bureau, and IAB Sgt. Stertzer called to request a meeting. At the meeting, he said Tampa Police Chief Bennie Holder would fire Officer M. for untruthfulness. In a sworn statement, the officer denied testifying he used radar. Sgt. Stertzer told me officers who make false statements under oath cannot testify in court; so, the officer must be fired. However, this is only true if the police department wants to fire an officer, as examples exist of Tampa officers making false sworn statements and not being fired. Sgt. Stertzer then claimed they had evidence I ran the stop sign, which was ridiculous, since they were firing Officer M. for untruthfulness over my ticket. Obviously, if acknowledging the officer fabricated my ticket, the Tampa Police Department would open the door for all other stop sign ticket victims to request second court hearings and refunds. The Tampa Police Department wanted to keep their proceeds.

I later obtained the IAB final report. It stated Officer M. was dismissed for untruthfulness and misuse of department equipment (radar), as follows:

*"You told your sergeant and corporal that you did not testify, or mention in court, anything about a radar unit during this court*

*hearing. This statement was untruthful. The court transcripts show where you made direct references to your use of radar; in fact, the citizen's entire defense was made on whether or not your attention was on the radar or the wheels of her vehicle."*

I later learned this was Tampa's second effort to fire Officer M. Their real issue with him was not untruthfulness over my traffic ticket, but they used my information to the finish the job. Subsequent to the officer's dismissal, new paperwork was generated and Officer M. was allowed to resign rather than be fired, supposedly after the police union intervened.

On the traffic ticket, I filed a motion for reconsideration to the court, attaching the IAB report that Officer M. was fired over my ticket. The same magistrate reopened my case, dismissed my ticket, and ordered a refund of the $47 in court fees.

My faculty colleague, John, experienced a different kangaroo court traffic magistrate. In 2005, John received a $140 ticket, but he found Florida statutes that made what he did legal, so he requested a traffic hearing. This was during the peak of Tampa's traffic tickets. With so many tickets issued, traffic magistrate hearings were no longer held at the courthouse, but instead at an abandoned shopping center, the *Floriland Mall*.[21]

At John's arraignment hearing, ticketed drivers were not individually called to enter their plea, as I had done. Instead, they were ordered to form two lines: one for those pleading "guilty" or "nolo contendere" and a second line for those pleading "not guilty." John reports the magistrate encouraged all to enter the "guilty line," as drivers would be wasting the court's time by seeking a final hearing, which the magistrate threatened would result in a larger penalty. Those entering the guilty/nolo contendere line arranged with court staff to pay their tickets while those in the "not guilty" line were given dates for a final hearing.

---

21 In St. Louis County, Missouri, one town uses someone's living room to hold court hearings.

Similar to my experience, at his final hearing, John reports the magistrate was finding everyone guilty. When it was his turn to testify, John explained the officer misrepresented the circumstances. He presented the relevant statutes, pictures of the road, and a diagram of circumstances. In addition, John's mother, who was with him when he received the ticket, attended and was prepared to affirm John's statements. The magistrate was disinterested and told John to show his diagram to the officer. He then contended John incriminated himself and moved on to the next case. John asked the court staff what had happened and was told the magistrate withheld adjudication and he must pay $55 in court costs. Once again, the court profited, yet the Tampa Police Department earned nothing.

By 2008, a Tampa newspaper reported this same traffic magistrate managed 60 or more cases in a single evening with most cases netting a "*quick guilty verdict.*" In addition to the fine, the "guilty" drivers paid an additional $30 in court costs and a $57.50 Clerk of Court fee—the added expense for requesting a hearing. The magistrate was quoted in the article, affirming the need for "*saying 'guilty' all the time*" is because he takes the officer at their word, since he had "*little reason to doubt their claims.*" Based on the sheer number of tickets, he should have known the City of Tampa had traffic ticket quotas that were resulting in fraud.

My second ticket was issued in 2000 and produced another kangaroo court experience, but with an actual judge. I had hired an attorney who requested a hearing with a judge, in order to avoid a kangaroo court traffic magistrate. My ticket was issued following the minor accident that resulted in a dented license plate with the officers estimating the damage to the other car as $500. The minor accident did not require a police investigation, but the Tampa Police Department expected an investigation and ticket nonetheless, because they were misinformed and incorrectly believed they were paid by insurance companies to investigate all crashes to identify an at-fault driver.

At the conclusion of the investigation, the training officer (Officer Bowden) told me I did not violate a traffic law, but his supervisor had ordered a ticket issued to me nevertheless. The ticket the supervisor ordered was for "careless driving" that misrepresented an "injury to another" occurred, even though no injuries occurred. Officer Bowden said Careless Driving is considered more serious by insurance companies, relative to Following Too Closely, as it is often used in crashes with major injuries or fatalities. The officer's supervisor had started working at the Tampa Police Department around the same time as Officer M., who was terminated over my first ticket. At the time, I assumed this was retaliation, but later learned the Tampa police required a ticket at every crash. Further, only the ticket reported an injury, as the crash report correctly reported no injuries and that medical assistance was not needed.

At the time of the ticket, Officer Bowden stated he did not identify a careless driving action on the ticket. He told me to inform the judge that a careless driving action was not documented, which would result in the ticket being dismissed, because the law requires the driving act deemed "careless" to be described and documented on the ticket. This proved correct. The Florida Supreme Court had ruled in *Robinson v. State, 152 So.2d 717* (Fla. 1934) that careless driving is a vague charge and therefore a ticket must document the driving behavior the officer deemed careless.[22] Thus, Officer Bowden followed his supervisor's order to write the careless driving ticket that misrepresented an injury, but did so in a manner that allowed for the ticket to be dismissed.

At the hearing, I told the judge my ticket did not identify the driving action deemed careless, but the judge did not care that it was incomplete per the Florida Supreme Court ruling, signaling this was another kangaroo court. I then explained the accident circumstances, which included that the afternoon of the minor accident had been the first rain of many months. The other driver attended and said it

---

22 The Florida Supreme Court had ruled it is "*impossible for the defendant to know what act or circumstance constituted the alleged infraction of the law....A defendant has the right to know from the language of the charge against him what conduct on his part is the basis of that charge.*"

had not rained.[23] The judge said his ruling would be based on whether or not the pavement was wet. He then shuffled through papers in front of him, which turned out to be the false crash report written by the rookie officer. The judge declared my statement about rain was not supported by the police. At the time, I did not know crash reports were used as secret testimony, so it was baffling why the judge claimed to have police testimony when an officer was not present. In court, I had the newspaper from the day following the accident that reported the afternoon rain as the first in many months, but the judge refused to review it. The judge withheld adjudication based on the false crash report and ordered $100 in court costs. Once again, the court profited while the Tampa Police Department earned $0.

I subsequently wrote to Tampa's police chief, asking to gain access to the training officer's (Officer Bowden's) knowledge of the circumstances. His aide, John Bennett, responded with a letter claiming they prohibit access to an officer's knowledge of the accident circumstances, and only the crash report can be accessed. Bennett contended the crash report was accurate, even though this turned out to be untrue. It became apparent why the Tampa Police Department and judges did not want officers to attend the hearings. When Officer Bowden was deposed in my federal lawsuit (5 years after my minor accident), he said it had been raining and the pavement was wet, which would have led to my ticket being dismissed. He also said careless driving may not be an appropriate charge and that he expected my ticket to be dismissed, because no one would attend to testify against me.

John Bennett's letter affirmed the Tampa police believed they were writing tickets over *fault* (who paid damages), as stated in his quotation that begins this chapter, whereas the police can only issue

---

23 When the other driver was deposed in my federal lawsuit, he explained that at the time of the traffic hearing he was planning to sue me for more money, even though my insurance company had paid him the $700 he requested for damages. He also said his attorney refused to file a lawsuit against me, despite his wishes. The man had previously sued another driver over a crash and was also sued for injuring another driver in a crash that occurred not long after he testified in my traffic ticket hearing.

a ticket for a traffic violation. Fault (who paid damages) is inadmissible in traffic ticket hearings. An officer would need to identify a traffic law (driving) violation in a traffic ticket court hearing. After receiving Bennett's letter, I requested the hearing transcript from the court in order to prove: a) the judge ignored that the ticket failed to document a careless driving action, b) the judge purported to have police testimony, despite an officer not attending the hearing, and c) the judge refused to review my newspaper evidence. I planned to file a complaint about the judge, as the local courthouse was under a federal investigation, which ultimately resulted in many local judges being ousted, including the Chief Judge. In response to my request for the transcript, I was told the court no longer records traffic ticket hearings, meaning it is not possible to prove what transpired at the hearing. Failure to record hearings is another element of a kangaroo court, as it is impossible to appeal based on what occurred at the hearing.

I called the Florida Attorney General's ethics office. A staffer said I was describing circumstances characteristic of small Florida towns, where *the police chief is the mayor's brother-in-law and they each own half the town.* He told me to call the Florida Department of Law Enforcement (FDLE), since they would assist me, as the AG's office only assists public officials. A local FDLE special agent advised me to obtain Tampa's written policies, which revealed the crash report was used as secret evidence at the hearing. I then ordered the crash report from the Tampa police and was given the 4-page report. It listed the pavement as dry and the weather as clear, despite the thunderstorm conditions. The rookie officer was untruthful about facts he could observe. The report had many other errors that were easy to prove as false.

I then hired Mr. Robert Merkle, the former U.S. Attorney for the Middle District of Florida. His firm had me file a motion for reconsideration, attaching the crash report and related documentation to prove the multiple errors on the crash report and alleging *intrinsic and extrinsic police fraud.* I also included a copy of the ticket to prove a careless driving action was not identified. The judge from the first hearing advised another judge to reopen my case, which occurred. My attorney subpoenaed Officer Bowden to the second hearing, but he did not attend. The judge asked me a few questions, complimented my efforts, dismissed the ticket, and ordered a refund of the $100 in court costs.

However, my auto insurance company then claimed the nearly $4,000 surcharge they had assessed, due to my ticket not having been initially dismissed, was *now* due to the crash report. They offered to refund the money *if* the Tampa police corrected the false entries on the report, which included documenting *why* the accident occurred. Mr. Merkle's firm submitted the documents to the Tampa Police Department that affirmed the crash report errors and asked for corrections to be made. Tampa's police attorney, Kirby Rainsberger, agreed the report had errors, but refused to correct them, even though Florida law makes it a crime to provide false information on a crash report. Rainsberger attributed the errors to the officer being a rookie, meaning he did not expect a rookie officer to write an accurate report. Mr. Rainsberger suggested resolving differences in court, which is what Officer Bowden had also recommended to me, but Officer Bowden's suggestion was for the purpose of stopping Tampa's ticket-at-every-crash policy.

Tampa's kangaroo traffic court later became even worse. In 2010, a ticketed driver asked her traffic attorney to enter a "not guilty" plea and request a hearing with a judge, since she could prove the Tampa traffic squad officer was not credible. Her attorney countered this was unwise, due to the judge assigned to her case. The attorney alleged that Tampa's police chief had met with the court's Chief Judge to ask that drivers be found guilty when pleading "not guilty," since the police need the money, as they have to pay officers to attend final hearings. In Tampa, officers are paid three hours of overtime when attending an off-duty traffic hearing. This means Tampa loses money on all final hearings that do not result in a "guilty" verdict. The attorney claimed the Chief Judge responded by sending a letter to traffic judges communicating the police chief's request.

The attorney further alleged the judge assigned to the driver's case was known to find all drivers guilty, if requesting a final hearing, with the penalty including the fine, court costs, and driver's license points. The attorney advised entering a "nolo contendere" plea, since this judge would then withhold adjudication and assess court costs only, which is what occurred. When seeking re-election, the judge had endorsements from two police unions, including the Tampa police union. Ethical standards for judges are set quite low in Florida, since endorsements from police unions openly signal a judge's bias in favor of the police. Ideally, it should be illegal for judges to accept endorsements from police unions, sheriffs or prosecutors.

I spoke with the traffic attorney and he told me he has personally witnessed the now predictable traffic court outcomes. He also knows another attorney who read the Chief Judge's letter, adding this court practice has ruined his business, due to the inability to access a fair hearing. While Tampa's traffic magistrates have been known to find nearly all drivers guilty, the traffic attorney alleged the same is true of this particular judge, if a ticketed driver requests a final hearing.

The police and court in Tampa, Florida are business partners in policing for profit. Apparently, there are no existing laws to prevent their collusion.

Meanwhile, the opposite of kangaroo courts also exists, *Sweetheart Deal Court*, which are court proceedings that benefit "special" people who receive a ticket or are charged with a crime. When a local Tampa judge began his position, he reported to the media that he was approached by another judge and informed that judges have a network whereby they inform one another of persons for whom they would like favorable consideration.

As an example of favorable treatment, in 2014, a jailed police informant gave a Tampa police sergeant permission to use her welfare benefits card, and the sergeant bought more than $300 in groceries for herself. The sergeant was fired and charged with food stamp fraud and grand theft. The former sergeant's attorney filed a motion for dismissal, claiming the sergeant did not know it was a crime to use the

welfare benefits of another. While the public has been told that ignorance of the law is no excuse, this tenet does not apply in *Sweetheart
Deal Court*. A judge threw out the sergeant's case, because she did not
know using someone else's welfare benefits was a crime. Meanwhile,
this same judge sentenced the police informant to 18 months in prison for fraud and grand theft over this very same offense.

The federal court in Tampa also exhibited *Sweetheart Deal Court*
regarding Judge Stringer, who was the traffic judge who wrote the
memo allowing the use of crash reports in court and who later became
an appellate court judge. While an appellate judge, he was charged
with bank fraud after a newspaper reported he aided a stripper in
hiding her income from the IRS. With the stripper's knowledge, the
judge had purchased a house in Hawaii under the pretense the down
payment was the judge's money, whereas it was the stripper's. The
dispute with the stripper arose after she accused the judge of making
purchases with her money absent her consent, e.g., a Mercedes Benz
car and Rolex watches for the judge and his wife. In return for the
judge pleading guilty, federal prosecutors agreed not to pursue other
charges, which suggests the former judge got to keep the Mercedes
Benz and Rolex watches. While bank fraud is a felony that carries a
maximum sentence of 30 years in prison, a federal judge in Tampa
sentenced former Judge Stringer to no prison time, 150 hours of
community service, and a $250 fine following his plea deal—a sweet-
heart deal for bank fraud.[24]

---

24 Robert O'Neill was the federal prosecutor who advocated for former Judge
Stringer's lenient sentence. Years earlier, in 2002, he was head of the public
corruption unit for the Middle District of Florida when I filed my complaint
about Tampa's ticket-at-every crash policy and the secret submission of false
crash reports to traffic court hearings, which is a practice Judge Stringer created.
My complaint was never investigated by Mr. O'Neill's unit, despite Assistant
U.S. Attorney Jeffrey Del Fuoco's attempt to do so. Mr. O'Neill eventually
became the U.S. Attorney for the Middle District of Florida.

# CHAPTER 7

# THE PROPRIETARY TRAFFIC SAFETY ESTABLISHMENT

## The Auto Insurance Industry

*"The best remedy for aggressive driving and crash prevention is traffic law enforcement. This is not only the local philosophy, but one which is nationwide."*

Sgt. John Bennett
Executive Aide to Tampa Police Chief Bennie Holder
September 11, 2000

John Bennett's statement above is incorrect. Traffic law enforcement (tickets) was not the means by which motor vehicle safety greatly improved over the past 50 years. However, Bennett's belief represents what some proprietary interests want law enforcement officers to believe—that safety is improved by writing more and more traffic tickets. This is not new news. It was revealed in the 1965 book by Ralph Nader, *Unsafe at Any Speed: The Designed in Dangers of the American Automobile*. Chapter 7 of his book is titled *The traffic safety establishment: Damn the driver and spare the car*. In it, Nader illustrated how the automobile and automobile insurance industries were generally not focused on traffic safety, but instead on their own revenues and profits. He also revealed the partnership between the auto insurance and the financial industry, since insurance companies invest premium revenues in the financial market, with insurers profiting more so from their investments than from underwriting profits.

Warren Buffet is the CEO of Berkshire Hathaway and one of the wealthiest people in the world. He admits that his insurance products, which include GEICO auto insurance and reinsurance ventures, have been excellent in creating revenue and profit for his company, in part due to "float." Float is the insurance premium revenue that can be invested once collecting premiums and prior to paying claims.

When a driver gets a ticket and points on their driver's license, there is no actual expense for an auto insurer and yet the insurance company is allowed to charge higher rates. Meanwhile, the premium increase from the points increases underwriting profits, as well as the funds available to the insurance company for investing in the market. Consequently, auto insurers have a financial interest in law enforcement officers writing more tickets, since it is an excuse for insurance companies to increase drivers' premiums.[25] It becomes obvious that the financial interests of auto insurance companies are directly contrary to the public. Drivers want to pay as little as possible for auto insurance, whereas insurance companies want growth in revenues and profits.

My attorney obtained the rates my auto insurance company had filed with the State of Florida, which allowed for decoding their point system. In 2000, the insurance increase due to driver's license points from a traffic ticket was 80% for three years, and assessed to the two drivers on the policy with the highest rates. For example, if a policy had a couple (two parents) and two teenage drivers, the surcharge would apply to the two teen drivers regardless of who received the ticket. The insurance terms were designed to maximize the increase from a ticket, rather than restrict the penalty to the driver who received the ticket. Also, a ticket does not equate to a driver being 80% more likely to file

---

25 Some insurance companies have purchased radar guns for police departments, which facilitates writing more speeding tickets.

a claim in each of the next three years, yet insurance companies are allowed to assess such ridiculous increases nonetheless.

The 80% increase works as follows. If a couple was paying $2,000 annually for auto insurance, absent a ticket, the total would be $6,000 over three years. A single ticket would create an 80% increase for both drivers, despite only one driver receiving a ticket, which totals an additional $4,800 in premiums over three years. Instead of paying $6,000, the couple would pay $10,800 over the three years. The additional $4,800 is underwriting profit for the auto insurer—money that can be invested in the market. Thus, traffic tickets create a wealth transfer from drivers to auto insurance companies.

The Insurance Institute for Highway Safety (IIHS) is funded by auto insurance companies and related professional associations. In 1965, Nader's book reported the IIHS advocates for traffic tickets (enforcement). This continues today, as IIHS staff insert themselves as educators to law enforcement officers, such as at Governor's Highway Safety Association's annual meetings. From my perspective, it is unethical for government agencies to spend taxpayer money to send public officials to conferences where proprietary interests, such as the IIHS and red-light traffic camera "front" groups (e.g., The National Campaign to Stop Red Light Running), feign as experts touting the importance of more and more traffic tickets, including automated enforcement. The Tampa police administration belief that tickets reduce crashes emanates from proprietary interests, and *not* from science. This sort of proprietary peddling is why police administrators, such as John Bennett, are unfamiliar with how motor vehicle safety *actually* improved.

Motor vehicle safety was one of the top 10 public health accomplishments of the 20th century. Since the 1960s, motor vehicle safety has improved through automobile engineering improvements, roadway engineering improvements, reducing driving under the influence (DUI), and increased safety belt use.[26] The latter two outcomes are

---

26 The CDC (Centers for Disease Control and Prevention) identified motor vehicle safety as one of the top 10 public health accomplishments of the 20th century.

improved by the threat of enforcement, whereby drivers do not drink and drive, and they use seat belts, to avoid being arrested or ticketed. The goal is *not* to have more DUI arrests and seat belt violation tickets, as this would mean drivers are impaired and not using seat belts.

In my federal lawsuit, a major dispute with the Tampa police was whether *fault* alone (who pays damages) constituted a traffic violation, recognizing Florida law does not allow fault to be used as evidence in traffic court hearings. Insurance companies, and not police officers, decide which driver will pay damages (fault) and any disputes are settled in civil lawsuits. In his book, Ralph Nader attributed the notion that "fault signals a traffic violation" to proprietary interests. He avowed the automobile and automobile insurance industries comprised a *private traffic safety establishment* that was *not* particularly focused on safety. The proprietary interests believed the occurrence of an accident implies a traffic violation, which Nader explained as follows: *The law embodies an invincible rationale: He had an accident; therefore, he violated the law.*[27] Nader concluded this focus was more "*a political strategy to defend special interests, than it is an empirical program to save lives and prevent injuries.*"

Nader went on to say crash reports conclude with "*the cause of the accident in terms of driver error,*" such that other causes of accidents and injuries are ignored. He noted that accident investigations are limited to "contributing circumstances" of the driver and do not consider other explanatory factors.[28] This proprietary perspective has been embraced by the Tampa police administration, with their focus being on *what* happened, and not *why* it happened. In 2007, Tampa police attorney Ursula Richardson wrote to my attorney, refusing to amend the false crash report. She explained the report reflects *what*

---

27 Nader also wrote the following about the proprietary interests: "*The reasoning behind this philosophy of safety can be summarized in this way: Most accidents are in the class of driver fault; driver fault is in the class of violated traffic laws; therefore, observance of traffic laws by drivers would eliminate most accidents.*"

28 Mr. Nader criticized this perspective as focusing exclusively on drivers for the purpose of "*exhorting him, watching him, judging him, punishing him, compiling records about his driving violations.*"

happened, but not *why* it occurred.[29] The Tampa police attorneys
never disagreed with why my accident occurred. They simply did
not want it documented on the crash report, meaning they did not
want a judge or my insurance company to know *why* the accident occurred. However, accident circumstances are considered in court and
by insurance companies, as evidenced by my insurance company's
willingness to refund nearly $4,000 if the Tampa police documented
the actual accident circumstances.

In his book, Nader also pointed out that some traffic laws are
very specific, such as provisions for passing a school bus, whereas others are quite vague, which allow for ticketing at every accident. His
example was reckless driving, which can *"cover almost any situation
that is not explicitly cited."* In other words, if a driver did not violate
a specific traffic law, such as following too closely, then a vague law
can be used, such as reckless or careless driving. Nader identified the
flaw in this argument is that some accidents occur for *other* reasons,
meaning all accidents do not occur due to a traffic law violation.

Thus, the notion that *fault* constitutes a traffic violation comes
from proprietary corporate interests and, if true, would result in a
ticket at every crash, since someone is responsible for paying damages
in every accident.

In my federal lawsuit, the Tampa police commander of patrol operations explained "careless driving" in his deposition. Captain Hugh
Miller responded to the question *"What's careless driving?"* as follows:
*"Unfortunately, a catchall, when a specific statute does not apply."* This is
the proprietary corporate perspective that Nader described in 1965.
Miller went on to say that if an accident occurs and a specific statute
does not apply, such as following too closely, then careless driving
is applicable. His understanding of the law is incorrect, as Florida

---

29 Attorney Richardson wrote: *"The narrative will remain unchanged because the
officer's narrative in the report accurately reflects that your client's vehicle crashed
into the rear of a stopped car and her explanation for why she hit a stopped vehicle
is not required to be noted on the crash report. The narrative appropriately reflects
what happened and not why it happened."*

case law requires an officer to specify a careless driving action on the ticket, and not just that an accident occurred.

In addition, Officer Jeffrey J. Thiel, who was the Tampa Police Department's Field Training Supervisor, said the following in his deposition in my lawsuit: "*I would say that when you look at the violation, whatever violation you're charging them with, say, following too closely or careless driving, a rear-end crash would fit almost every instance. I don't see how it would not.*" Apparently, Officer Thiel did not understand the law, since he believes every rear-end crash constitutes following too closely and careless driving, regardless of the following distance or whether a careless driving action was identified. Likewise, he did not understand the math related to braking and stopping, as understanding the math explains why some rear-end accidents are unavoidable.

However, the notion that *fault* is synonymous with a traffic violation did not apply to Tampa's police chiefs or the supervisor who ordered my ticket. In 2000, five months after my minor accident, Police Chief Holder caused a rear-end crash, absent any mitigating circumstances. It resulted in the City of Tampa paying $3,245 in damages to the driver of the rear-ended car. Chief Holder did not receive a traffic ticket. The cause of his crash was not Following Too Closely or Careless Driving, but instead was listed as "Other." "Other" was explained on the crash report narrative as follows: "*was unable to come to a complete stop and struck the rear of VEH#2 with its front.*" A Tampa police sergeant gave me Chief Holder's crash report to prove a double standard existed.

In addition, the very same supervisor who had ordered my ticket in a minor, non-injury crash previously caused an accident himself while driving in the rain. When attempting to change lanes, his police car spun, left the roadway, and hit and damaged a guardrail. He did not receive a ticket and instead was referred for disciplinary action by the Tampa Police Department. The conclusion of the related police investigation was that he failed "*to operate his vehicle in a careful and prudent manner under adverse weather conditions.*" Some law enforcement agencies contend that facing disciplinary action is a more serious consequence for officers than receiving a traffic ticket, which is their excuse for not ticketing officers. However, the disciplinary action taken was listed as "VOID," meaning there were no consequences for the officer after causing the single vehicle accident that damaged a guardrail.

On January 5, 2005, while my federal lawsuit was ongoing, Tampa Police Chief Stephen Hogue was driving to work in his police car when he caused a 4-car pile-up. He rear-ended a Volkswagen Jetta, hitting it with such force that it ran into the back of an Acura, which skidded into the back of a pick-up truck. Damages to the Chief's police vehicle and the Jetta were extensive. The police chief admitted to "looking over his shoulder," not realizing traffic had stopped. He received a ticket for Following Too Closely, which should have netted four points on his driver's license and a very large, multi-year auto insurance increase. And it should be noted he could *not* attend driving school to avoid the driver's license points, because he had already attended driving school a few months earlier after receiving a ticket following a minor one-vehicle accident, while posturing (for purposes of my lawsuit) that every crash necessitates a ticket, regardless of how minor. However, his second ticket for the rear-end crash never appeared on the Clerk of Court website—it simply disappeared—which was no doubt good news for the police chief and his personal auto insurance rates.

In my federal lawsuit, Tampa police administrators and City of Tampa attorneys were attempting to advance auto insurance interests by overriding Florida law to make *fault* a basis for ticketing (albeit not applicable to themselves), with careless driving as the ticket to issue when a specific traffic law was not violated. Federal case law would trump Florida law, so they were attempting to change public policy in the Middle District of Florida to advantage auto insurance companies. Also consistent with Nader's statements about proprietary interests, City of Tampa attorneys did not believe crash reports should explain why an accident occurred. Thus, Tampa officials were advancing the proprietary corporate interests that Ralph Nader had described back in 1965.

The financial advantage to auto insurers from Tampa's ticket-at-every-crash policy was evidenced in the rates my insurance company filed with the State. At the time, a conviction on a ticket would create a 3-year 80% increase to the two most expensive drivers on the policy (my husband and teenaged son). Filing a claim to repair the cars would create an additional 40% increase for three years, but could not be assessed if the ticket was dismissed, as occurred in my case. Having both a ticket and a claim created another 15% increase from losing a "preferred" insurance status. Thus, if merely paying the $90 careless driving ticket, my auto insurance premium increase would have been 135% for three years, which was an $11,000 insurance increase over three years. The means by which auto insurers profit from tickets and minor crashes becomes obvious. When small claims are made for minor crashes, the insurance surcharges and penalties can greatly exceed the amount paid for the claim. This may explain why the IIHS advocates for red-light cameras, since these cameras are associated with a 50% to 60% increase in rear-end crashes. The multi-year penalty for filing a claim from such crashes can greatly exceed the amount the insurance company paid to repair damages.

The IIHS is a champion of automated enforcement (red-light cameras and speed cameras). If the goal is to produce as many tickets as possible to justify insurance premium increases, then automating the issuance of tickets should greatly increase auto insurance revenues and profits. The IIHS conducts its own research to peddle the notion that cameras are effective in reducing crashes and fatalities. Meanwhile, my colleagues and I have published replications of two IIHS red-light camera studies to prove their findings are not credible. In reality, scientific research concludes red-light cameras are associated with significant *increases* in crashes and injuries, as drivers are prone to slam on the brakes at camera sites, which is a hazardous driving behavior. Further, the cameras do not reduce red-light running crashes and injuries, because they have no impact on unintentional (accidental) red light running.

Since crashes provide a reason for auto insurers to charge drivers more, increasing minor crashes should result in increasing premiums, absent any loss to insurers. For example, prior to having red-light cameras in Tampa, total auto insurance premiums paid were trending downward after my lawsuit, as Tampa had abandoned its ticket-at-every-crash policy, coupled with the economic downturn. In the first year of red-light camera use, auto insurance premiums paid in Tampa increased. The cameras provided no savings for the public, as drivers paid about $11 million for Tampa's 69,000 camera tickets issued in the first year and total auto insurance premiums paid in Tampa increased by another $11 million—costing drivers $22 million more.

For consumers, the problem with insurance stems from inadequate regulation at federal and state levels, which advantages the auto insurance and financial industries. In reality, current laws and regulations regarding insurance are contrary to capitalism and the free market. The auto insurance industry should be stagnant or in decline based on the product life cycle. In the 1950s and 1960s, the auto insurance industry grew as more people drove cars, and 1-car households became 2-car or 3-car households, reflecting market growth that increased auto insurance revenues, due to more drivers and vehicles. However, this reached a plateau.

In addition, beginning in the mid-1960s, motor vehicle safety was advanced, which reduced serious and fatal crashes, and hence the insurance premiums needed to pay large claims. Consistent with these trends, auto insurance premiums stagnated during the 1990s, as revenues, profits, and stock prices were flat. This is how the product life cycle works. As safety further advanced, auto insurance should continue to stagnate, no longer a cash cow.

However, this did not occur, in part, due to the McCarran-Ferguson Act of 1945 that gave insurance companies the ability to engage in practices that would be deemed "price fixing," if not for the exemptions provided by this federal law.[30] In 2000, auto insurance

---

30 Appendix C provides an analysis by the GAO explaining the provisions for price fixing by insurance companies.

companies responded to stagnant premiums by creating new pricing tools. Instead of putting drivers into four or five underwriting categories, they now surcharge or penalize for everything imaginable: tickets, claims, credit ratings, being in a crash, but *not at fault*, inquiring about filing a claim, despite not filing a claim, and who knows what else, *because the law does not require insurers to tell us*, meaning we are uniformed about how to lower our insurance premiums. When I asked my insurance company for the specifics, they told me it was proprietary information.

So much for the product life cycle applying to insurance. Automobile insurers in the U.S. transitioned from stagnant revenues and profits in the 1990s to achieve record gains, despite motor vehicle safety further improving. Around 1999 to 2000, three events occurred to advance auto insurance financial interests.

1. The insurance industry developed new pricing tools to increase opportunities to justify premiums increases from tickets, crashes and other factors.

2. The IIHS began peddling "automated enforcement," e.g., red-light cameras that are associated with large increases in rear-end crashes and no change in red-light running crashes or injuries.

3. Florida law was changed to incentivize police officers to write more tickets in order to receive "extra" police pension benefits. Police administrators in Florida were co-opted to act as business partners with insurers, creating enormous expense for Floridians. From 2000 to 2004, Florida experienced a large auto insurance rate increase, moving up five places to become the sixth most expensive state in the nation for auto insurance.

Unfortunately, auto insurance is contrary to principles of capitalism for reasons in addition to price fixing. First, in the free market, people choose what they want to purchase. In contrast, state law requires drivers to purchase auto insurance. Proprietary interests posture that "driving is a privilege," which suggests one does not need to drive. This is untrue, since cities such as Tampa lack a public transportation infrastructure, making cars a necessity.

Auto insurance also defies principles of capitalism, because we do not understand the price, terms, or whether or when a claim would be paid. The price should be explained, including the base price due to age, gender and address, as well as each added fee for other factors, such as points on a driver's license, filing a claim, asking about filing a claim, being in a crash but not at fault, and everything else for which insurance companies assess surcharges or penalties. The *basis for an insurance policy's price should be fully disclosed to consumers prior to purchase.*

Since the free market assumes consumers understand the price and product, consumers should be informed of all the potential add-on costs from factors insurance companies use to increase rates, otherwise it is impossible to compare among policies to choose the best option. For example, insurance companies should disclose the percentage increase that would occur if filing a claim, as well as how long the penalty would be assessed, recognizing in Florida it varies from three to seven years. Policies should disclose the percentage increase that would occur if getting points on one's driver's license, as well as points from a second ticket. I know someone who experienced a 100% premium increase (doubling) for three years, after filing a claim for a minor rear-end accident. One cannot know if another policy had a lower percentage, if these terms are not disclosed at the time of purchase. At present, auto insurance is equivalent to buying "a pig in a poke."

Federal law should require such disclosures. Insurance companies need to reveal the terms, so consumers can use the information to select one policy over another. Further, there should be a guarantee of when a claim will be paid, e.g., within 30 days from the date the claim is filed, recognizing insurance companies have a financial incentive to defer paying large claims, because the money is invested for their own financial gain.

Insurance companies were further advantaged by the McCarran-Ferguson Act, since it allows state governments, instead of the federal government, to regulate insurance. This is preferred by insurance companies, given state regulation is less rigorous, which was also explained in Nader's 1965 book. This is evidenced by the federal regulation of health insurance under Obamacare. Private health insurance companies must spend 80 to 85 cents of every premium dollar on health care, thereby restricting funds available for administration and profit. In contrast, states are not required to set such expectations for auto insurers. In Florida, at last reporting in 2006, auto insurers were spending about 60 cents of each premium dollar on claims, giving themselves 40% of each premium dollar for administration and profit.

In Florida, state regulation is further problematic for consumers, since the rates filed with the State are not enforced. For example, Florida law prohibits red-light camera tickets from being used in setting auto insurance rates. When I asked the State insurance office if insurance companies were nonetheless doing so, a regulator responded that they assumed so and told me to ask my insurance company. When my attorney informed my insurance company they needed to refund the 40% surcharge they had assessed, consistent with the rates they filed with the State, they refused. My insurance agent told me no one would make them refund the money, even if violating the rates filed with the State.

In the interest of consumers, the use of credit ratings in setting insurance rates should be prohibited by federal and state laws, and enforced. As an example of this perversity, one of my children received a "teaser" quote from GEICO auto insurance. When following up, he learned he could not have the rate due to a low credit rating. His credit rating was low only because he earned his money before spending it, meaning he did not need credit cards or loans. He was informed he could improve his credit rating by using credit cards, and was subsequently sent an application for an American Express card. Berkshire Hathaway owns GEICO and is a major shareholder in American Express, making this a conflict of interest. My son could have a lower GEICO insurance rate if allowing a company, such as

American Express, to profit from purchases he makes on their credit card. Federal law should ban the use of credit ratings in setting insurance premiums, because consumers should not be penalized because they do not use credit cards or need loans. In particular, lower income persons are more likely to use cash, such that allowing auto insurers to use credit ratings to justify premium increases ultimately discriminates against lower income persons.

Until Congress reverses the perverse provisions in the Mc-Carran-Ferguson Act and creates sound federal laws for insurance companies, the public should expect executives in the insurance and financial industries to become richer, while the middle class erodes, as a wealth transfer is occurring from the public to insurance companies, as well as the financial institutions where insurance companies invest their proceeds.[31] It is a zero sum game: as the rich get richer, others become less prosperous. From 2000 to 2009, auto insurers made Tampa drivers pay an extra $1 billion to them, relative to the prior 10 years—a $1 billion gain for them at a $1 billion loss to Tampa drivers. As motorists are required to pay more to insurance companies, they have less money to save, invest, or spend on goods and services in other sectors. Policing for profit is an obvious means for auto insurance companies to amass wealth, which is mutually beneficial for the financial sector.

In addition, financial firms can profit directly from policing for profit. For example, Goldman Sachs is a major shareholder in the red-light camera vendor American Traffic Solutions. It is cyclic in terms of revenue generation: Berkshire Hathaway, which owns GEICO auto insurance, is a major shareholder in Goldman Sachs. Goldman Sachs is a major shareholder in the red-light camera vendor American Traffic Solutions, whose investment helps fund American

31 In the book *Aftershock*, Robert B. Reich, former Secretary of Labor, explained that the deregulation of Wall Street has allowed the finance industry to prosper. He wrote in 2010 that, *"financial and insurance companies accounted for 40 percent of American corporate profits,"* whereas it had been only 10 percent during the Great Prosperity (mid 1940s to late 1970s).

Traffic Solutions in peddling red-light cameras to communities interested in increasing revenue under the false pretense of safety. This not only profits the vendor and its investors, e.g., Goldman Sachs, but also allows GEICO to increase auto insurance rates, due to the increase in rear-end crashes from cameras. These cameras are "gratuitous privatization" under the pretense of public service, creating a wealth transfer from the public to vendors, their financial investors, and auto insurers.

# CHAPTER 8

# THE PROPRIETARY PUBLIC SAFETY ESTABLISHMENT

## Other Corporate Interests

*"In the councils of government, we must guard against the acqui-sition of unwarranted influence, whether sought or unsought, by the military-industrial complex. The potential for the disastrous rise of misplaced power exists and will persist. We must never let the weight of this combination endanger our liberties or dem-ocratic processes. We should take nothing for granted. Only an alert and knowledgeable citizenry can compel the proper mesh-ing of the huge industrial and military machinery of defense with our peaceful methods and goals, so that security and liberty may prosper together."*

President Dwight D. Eisenhower
1960

In 1960, President Eisenhower warned of the misplaced influence of the corporate military-industrial complex, having the potential to *"endanger our liberties or democratic processes."* Those who work for and/or support the existence of this complex profit from war and heightened surveillance systems, which are funded by taxpayers. Then, in 1965, Ralph Nader warned of the corporate *proprietary traffic safety establishment* that was not focused on traffic safety. Similar to the military-industrial complex, they focus on their own revenues and profits, which are largely generated by citizens paying insurance increases. Since then, other types of corporations have emerged to advance a *proprietary public safety establishment*, using tactics similar to their predecessors by influencing public policy, while often endangering personal liberties and democratic processes, as President Eisenhower warned. Just like the proprietary traffic safety establishment, the *proprietary public safety establishment* targets citizens as "revenue sources," while in partnership with government.

The "business approach" to public safety entails corporations inserting themselves in all aspects of the justice system, while conducting some activities directly contrary to public safety and fairness. The *proprietary public safety establishment* profits from increasing the number of citizens who are charged with or convicted of violating a law. For example, they provide court collection services whereby vendors profit from increased convictions. They offer private prisons and prison management services, including vendors for inmate food services, snack concessions, and medical services, along with private probation services. In addition, private companies insert themselves as vendors in public-private ventures to advance revenues from parking meters, fire departments, emergency medical services, and toll roads. A wide variety of private corporations profit from such policing for profit tactics to create a wealth transfer from the public to these private companies.

At the time of my federal lawsuit, I found one company, Affiliated Computer Services (ACS), that provided a complete "justice system" supply line. ACS issued traffic tickets from red-light cameras, speed cameras, and toll road violation cameras. Then, their court system for traffic case management allowed for recording "*extensive personal and vehicle data.*" ACS also provided court management IT and court collection services, selling *Agile*Court and *Agile*Jury systems to courts for docket and jury management, as well as a system to automate court case management. They advertised that court business processes differed and courts are in a "state of flux." ACS explained their products are "*designed to provide courts with the most flexible products on the market, giving you what your court needs most: agility.*"[32] While their IT systems claimed to meet court standards, their advertising suggested the possibility of tampering with the programming at the local level.

Their jury management system allowed for selecting jury pools, designed to be "*flexible, customizable, and expandable.*" Apparently, all courts are not looking for similar jury pools, so some need to be customized. For instance, my attorney had a client waging a federal lawsuit against the City of Tampa police over excessive force. He wondered how the jury pool could include so many people with relatives in law enforcement. Perhaps the jury pool had been "customized." ACS advertised their jury management system was used by the federal court and "*puts business logic in the hands of business experts.*" This was accomplished, their web site conveyed, by helping "*courts adapt to changing needs by updating business rules directly.*" Their marketing emphasized the word "business," as if the court is a business. It is unclear what oversight exists regarding these ACS court-related products, or those sold by similar vendors, if courts can make programming changes to these IT systems at the local level.

Finally, ACS provided collection services for tickets and penalties assessed in court. In other words, they profit from issuing tickets, from their products to manage court rules, dockets and jury pools, and from collecting fines and fees assessed from convictions. ACS had a financial stake in having more tickets, more court cases, and more convictions by having a financial interest in collections.

In an approach to "generate income" from motorists, ACS and other private vendors persuade public officials to use their camera technology to automate the issuance of traffic tickets. Cameras have been developed to detect stop sign violations, in addition to red light running, speeding, passing a school bus, and toll road violations. Private camera vendors have a financial incentive to create as many offenders as possible. These vendors currently participate in all three

---

32 ACS was purchased by Xerox in 2010. Xerox continues to sell *Agile*Court and *Agile*Jury, but no longer emphasizes agility and customizability on their website.

branches of local government. First, they act in the legislative branch by drafting local ordinances to allow cameras, stipulating terms and provisions to their own advantage. Camera vendors also act in the executive branch of government by choosing where to locate cameras, influencing yellow light timings, and often deciding who receives a ticket. Then, vendors have IT systems to manage court processes and collections, thereby functioning in the judicial branch. In Florida, the privatization of red-light camera enforcement became the subject of a class action lawsuit. The plaintiffs' attorneys accused private vendors of using police powers that were restricted to counties and municipalities. In 2015, the attorneys wrote, "*The vendors' employees—and not local law enforcement officers—control almost the entire law enforcement process.*"[33]

Increasing camera ticket violations can be achieved by roadway engineering defects, such as shortening the yellow light timing at red-light camera sites or using arbitrary speed limit reductions to increase the number of speed camera tickets. Shortened yellow light timings ultimately discriminates against individuals who require a longer stopping distance, such as the elderly, who have a slower average perception/reaction time to braking, and lower income persons, whose vehicles are more likely to have inexpensive tires that require a longer stopping distance. When such drivers cannot stop in time, they will receive a camera ticket when entering the intersection just after the traffic signal turns red, even for violations that are not visible to the human eye. Red-light camera vendors view video in slow motion to find drivers who entered an intersection a fraction of a second after the signal turned red, because their goal is to maximize tickets.

The problem with red-light cameras was explained in a 2001 analysis from the U.S. House Majority Leader' office (Dick Armey). In 2000, federal standards were changed to reduce the minimum

---

33 Subsequently, in August 2015, the City of Tampa was sued over its red-light camera program, which alleged it is unconstitutional because the City was delegating their power to ticket drivers to a private company (American Traffic Solutions), in violation of Florida law.

yellow light timings that must be set at traffic signals. When shorter timings are used, a dilemma zone is created, where drivers cannot stop in time and will enter the intersection on a red light. This change (reducing yellow light timings) was essential to make red-light camera programs profitable, as the shorter yellow light timings increase red-light running and, hence, camera tickets and profits. The analysis also explained the IIHS was providing the research that concluded cameras are effective, but they were *failing* to report the large increases in rear-end crashes at camera sites.[34]

The Federal Highway Administration (FHWA) was created in 1966, a year after Ralph Nader's book (*Unsafe at Any Speed*) was published, and it has been a leader in advancing motor vehicle safety. However, it appears corporate interests infiltrated the FHWA by 2000. This is evidenced by federal standards endorsing shorter minimum yellow light timings, which again, allow red-light camera programs to be profitable. Further, although red-light cameras are associated with increases in crashes and injuries, the FHWA began promoting cameras after Norman Mineta became Secretary of Transportation from 2001 to 2006. Prior to becoming Secretary of Transportation, Mineta had been a congressman who subsequently became a corporate executive with Lockheed Martin, which had a red-light camera division that was sold to ACS. During Mineta's tenure as Secretary of Transportation, in 2005, the FHWA produced and peddled an unsound research study that created the appearance red-light cameras were effective, while the FHWA also failed to disseminate two sound studies (funded by the FHWA) that concluded cameras were a *detriment* to safety. The credible Virginia study found red-light cameras were associated with a 30% increase in crashes and an 18% increase in injury crashes. It also reported no significant change in red-light running crashes or injury crashes, which is likely because cameras do not impact accidental (unintentional) red-light running.

---

34 The report summarized the problem as follows. "*There's a hidden tax being levied on motorists today. In theory, this tax is only levied on those who violate the law and put others in danger. But the reality is that the game has been rigged. And we're all at risk.*"

The FHWA continues to post its unsound red-light camera study to its website, even though my colleagues and I have published critiques explaining why their study is not credible evidence of camera effectiveness. In fact, the *real* findings from this FHWA study are as follows: no significant change in crashes or injury crashes was found, but a higher percentage of crashes were fatal or had incapacitation injuries. The FHWA is not telling the truth about red-light camera effectiveness.[35]

More recently, the Centers for Disease Control and Prevention (CDC) also began peddling red-light cameras as an effective intervention. They also cite the flawed 2005 FHWA study described above. It is unfortunate the CDC and FHWA pander to proprietary interests. Regardless of the advocacy from these two federal agencies, as jurisdictions gain experience with cameras, programs are being terminated, e.g., about 60 cities in California and many in Florida.

In addition, private corporations provide other services to courts, such as electronic monitoring of offenders, continuous alcohol monitoring of alcohol offenders, and ignition interlocks for DUI offenders. These technologies may be viewed positively by public officials, when clients pay directly for the services, at no cost to the court. The private companies have a financial incentive to increase use of their technology.

Further, private companies offer probation services for persons who cannot afford the fine from their arrest and need a payment

---

35 The 2005 FHWA study is flawed for the following reasons. First, the authors reviewed the results of 15 camera programs and then selected 7 of the 15 to analyze, because they had the most favorable outcomes, which is selection bias. The 8 cameras programs with the least favorable outcomes were excluded from the analysis. More importantly, the study did *not* find a safety benefit from cameras, as suggested. The study concluded angle crashes decreased by 25 percent and rear-end crashes increased by 15 percent, purportedly a positive tradeoff, since angle crashes tend to be more severe than rear-end crashes. However, rear-end crashes are more frequent and the study failed to report changes in *total* crashes and injuries, which can be tallied from the results (page 63). The tally reveals no significant change occurred in total crashes or injury crashes, despite studying 370 site years of red-light cameras. Significantly, the study reported crash severity *increased* following camera use since a larger percentage of crashes were fatal and incapacitating injury crashes. Further, crashes specific to red-light running were not analyzed.

plan. Similar to the technologies above, courts may view this positively, since the offender pays the private probation company directly, costing the court nothing. However, private companies, used for court-approved debt collection, have created onerous fees to low income persons, resulting in costs that are many times the initial fine. This occurs because these private companies assess their own start-up and monthly fees. Any payment made is first allocated to the private company's fees, leaving the original fine unpaid with monthly fees continuing to accrue. A lawsuit ensued after a woman could not pay one company's minimum fee requirements and she was sent to jail as a consequence. The judge found the practice unconstitutional, referring to it as a *debtors' prison* and a *sanctioned extortion racket*.

Nonetheless, private probation companies have profited from low income persons who cannot afford to pay their modest fines. In reality, such proprietary companies are unnecessary, since courts can opt to offer community service to low income persons, as a means of paying their fines. However, courts that are policing for profit want the cash and will elect, instead, to use private probation companies.

Florida pays private prison vendors per-inmate-per-day, thus creating an incentive (for the vendor) to have as many inmates as possible—a possible deterrent to time off for good behavior. Florida also guarantees a 90% occupancy rate to private prison vendors. Proprietary vendors can also seek to minimize the cost of providing services to inmates. For example, in 2008, the Florida prison system's private food vendor was fined for inadequate staffing, insufficient food, slow service, and making inmates sick—*don't eat the chili!* Profits took precedence over adequate food service for inmates. More recently, Florida's medical care for prisoners was criticized as inadequate. It was reported that 320 inmates died in Florida prisons in 2014; however, some deaths were attributed to other factors, such as excessive force. Nonetheless, it is in the financial interest of prison and jail vendors to have as many inmates as possible, while keeping their costs as low as possible, even if it negatively impacts those being "served."

As an example of the perverse incentives, in Tampa, a man was jailed by sheriff deputies after a minor car accident. The man complained of being unable to move and was arrested, because he did not follow the deputies' order to get out of his vehicle. It turned out the man was unable to move because he'd had a stroke. Similarly, nurses from the jail's medical vendor failed to recognize the stroke symptoms. After three days of malingering in the jail, unable to move, the man was transported to a hospital, where he died. This reveals a conflict of interest. The medical vendor was paid about $20 per-inmate-per-day, such that a financial incentive existed to not transport the man to the hospital. A nurse from this vendor had previously made national news with the following "joke": "*We save money because we skip the ambulance and bring them right to the morgue.*" In Tampa, the jail's medical vendor ultimately settled with the man's family for $800,000, while the sheriff and emergency medical service settled for $200,000.

A similar scenario occurred with sheriff deputies in Pinellas County, Florida. In 2013, a 41-year-old man was arrested for DUI. He told the deputy he was not feeling well, but nonetheless was taken to jail, where the nurse documented he "*had generalized jaundice from head to toe.*" The man did not have a criminal record, other than his current DUI arrest. Due to state laws associated with a DUI arrest, the man was required to be held in custody for 8 hours. If the County or medical vendor transported him to the hospital within this 8-hour period, they would be responsible for the ambulance and hospital expenses, since he was in the sheriff's custody. As such, they planned to transport him to the hospital once the 8 hours had concluded, whereby he would be released and the ambulance and hospital expense would no longer accrue to the County or vendor. The man, who was married and father to four children, died in his jail cell before the 8 hours concluded, due to heart and liver issues. Ultimately, they transported him to the morgue, rather than to a hospital.

Parking meters provide another example of an emerging "business partnership" between public officials and corporations. In 2009, an MSNBC news report titled, "*Inside the Cut-Throat World of Parking Tickets,*" detailed the corporate perspective of this public-private partnership. A parking meter vendor explained they perceive government as ineffective in maximizing the return on investment (ROI) of its assets, and that the private sector is stepping in to help government attain the greatest possible earnings from its assets. The example given was parking meters, where private vendors would know to charge higher prices and never miss an opportunity for a parking ticket by using technology to identify expired meters. The vendor seemed to believe government should maximize parking meter revenue, with the vendor taking a share of the proceeds. Not surprisingly, the vendor reported the first thing a private company will do is raise prices, thereby producing more fee and fine revenue. This perspective suggests government exists for the purpose of *maximizing the amount of money taken from the public.*

The flaw in this public-private business partnership model is it ignores who owns the assets from which the private company is attempting to profit. While vendors seek to assess fines, fees and other charges to the public, *the public paid for the assets.* With government assets, citizens are the shareholders who paid for these assets, including police officers, fire fighters, parking spaces, parking meters, and roads. These assets should be managed to maximize value *for the public,* the shareholders who paid for them, as occurs in the corporate world.

Further, the fine and fee method of taxation is inefficient, since it costs taxpayers more than efficient taxation methods, such as income, property, gas or sales taxes. Efficient taxation methods do not entail a private company pilfering a share of the proceeds. For example, in 2015, it was revealed that Tampa receives 10% of the local share of their red-light camera revenue, while the vendor (American Traffic Solutions) collects 90%, making cameras an extraordinarily inefficient way to raise revenue for the City of Tampa.

"Firefighting for profit" also exists. Some vendors offer a public-private partnership to charge victims who use fire department services, such as a fire truck responding to a traffic crash. Prices vary by type of service. For example, the price for a fire truck responding to a minor crash would cost less than an extrication using the "jaws of life." Thus, the public pays for the fire department through taxes, and then a private vendor becomes the collection agency, setting prices as high as possible, while charging people who use fire department services, even though the public already paid for these resources.

Toll roads are yet another public-private venture. In 2009, a Wall Street Journal editorial titled, *Toll Roads Are Paved with Bad Intentions*, explained the flaw in government partnering with corporations, relative to converting interstate highways into toll roads:

> *It's a harsh, competitive world out there, and governments all over the world are racing one another to turn their infrastructure into investment opportunities... But there's good reason to be reluctant to privatize. It doesn't take an MBA to figure out that we didn't build our interstate highways in order to create opportunities for venture capitalists. The purpose was public service.*

The peculiarity with interstate toll roads is that taxpayers fund the interstate through taxes and then a private vendor charges motorists to use the interstate that motorists already paid for.

Auto insurers and some other corporate proprietary interests obviously profit from the "business approach" to public safety. Private corporations are quietly inserting themselves into a wide variety of services in all branches of government; not just as outsourced services, but also in dictating, if not heavily influencing, policies, practices and prices. It is in the financial interest of these proprietary corporate interests to *encourage public officials to believe they are running a business with the goal of maximizing revenue.*

They are *wrong*, however, since public officials should be creating value (public service). Value does not occur by creating a wealth transfer from citizens to public-private partnerships, ultimately creating wealth for private corporations. This reveals a reckless and costly hazard of privatizing public services, since private companies seek continuous revenue growth, regardless of whether it is good for the public.

# CHAPTER 9

# MY FEDERAL KANGAROO
# COURT EXPERIENCE

## A Tale of Falsities and Omissions

*"Unless a court issues a declaration of rights, the parties will not
know whether Defendants' policies and practices are unconstitutional and there will continue to be disputes and controversies
concerning this issue."*

Joseph Magri (my attorney)
*Orban v. City of Tampa*
Filed on August 19, 2004

Meanwhile, I landed in the middle of a kangaroo court with
my federal lawsuit. As will be clearly shown, my own experience provides evidence that an individual federal judge can advance
proprietary corporate interests by engaging in falsities and omissions,
absent any consequences.

In my case, the federal district judge, Steven Merryday, attempted
to advantage automobile insurance financial interests by endorsing
Tampa's practices, whereas the appellate judges derailed his attempt,
but also assured that the truth about Tampa's perverse police practices would never be disclosed to the public in a jury trial.[36] My lawsuit

---

36 The judges' rulings are posted on-line at www.highwayrobberytampa.com under the link to 'Cast of Characters.'

provides evidence that higher standards are needed to assure honesty and integrity among federal district and appellate judges.

Prior to my federal lawsuit, the officials and agencies that refused to investigate my complaint regarding the Tampa police policies, in the order pursued, were as follows: Tampa's Police Chief, Internal Affairs Bureau, Mayor, and City Councilman Bob Buckhorn (who was the Public Safety liaison at the time), the Florida Attorney General's office, a Florida Department of Law Enforcement (FDLE) supervisor, the State Attorney's office, the U.S. Attorney's public corruption unit, and CALEA, which accredits the Tampa Police Department.[37] An FDLE special agent had advised me in pursuing a complaint through most of these persons and agencies. In addition, a Florida Highway Patrol Captain in Tallahassee explained the State laws that the Tampa Police Department policies violated, which were numerous. For example, the Captain said it would be a "color of law" crime (felony) for a supervisor to order an investigating officer to write a ticket after the officer's investigation concluded probable cause did not exist to write a ticket.

My attorney, Joseph Magri,[38] filed my federal lawsuit *Orban v. City of Tampa, Florida* in the U.S. District Court for the Middle District of Florida on August 19, 2004. It alleged the City of Tampa issued tickets absent probable cause in accident investigations and fabricated related crash reports to raise revenue for the Police Pension Fund in violation of rights under the Fourth and Fourteenth Amendment of the U.S. Constitution. My lawsuit, or complaint as they call it, began with the general allegations from my experience and the remedial efforts

---

37 CALEA (Commission on Accreditation for Law Enforcement Agencies) standards require an investigation of all complaints. The CALEA site visit report documented that my complaint was investigated by the Tampa Police Department and the officers were disciplined, which is untrue. This reveals CALEA accreditation is not a genuine accountability system for law enforcement agencies. The CALEA representative informed me their "client" is the police chief. She declined to provide the documentation that my complaint was investigated, and told me to request it from the police chief. The Tampa Police Department told me that my complaint was never investigated.

38 Mr. Magri was Robert Merkle's law partner and continued my case after Mr. Merkle passed away in 2003. He was also a former federal prosecutor, serving as Chief Assistant U.S. Attorney under Mr. Merkle, and later as Acting U.S. Attorney for the Middle District of Florida.

attempted. It explained my nearly $4,000 auto insurance increase due to the false crash report, as well as the State law that creates the auto insurance kick-back to "extra" police pension benefits. It referenced the experiences of others who alleged Tampa police ticket fraud, stating the policies and practices not only affect me, but all others who may be ticketed in Tampa—"thousands of people."

My lawsuit was a 2-count complaint. Count 1 alleged Malicious Prosecution, as the citation was issued with legal malice. Count 2 pertained to the City violating my due process rights.[39] The declarations made identified 11 Tampa Police Department practices as illegal.[40] The last statement of the complaint was, *"Plaintiff demands trial by jury of all issues so triable."*

---

39 Mr. Magri wrote: *"An actual controversy exists between the Plaintiff and Defendants as to whether Defendants' policies, practices and customs in issuing traffic citations and traffic crash reports and presenting traffic citations without reasonable and probable grounds for the purpose of raising revenue for the Police Pension Fund violates the Plaintiff's rights under the Fourth and Fourteenth Amendments of the Unites States Constitution."*

40 The 11 declarations are as follows:
1. The City's policies, practices and customs to write a traffic citation without reasonable and probable grounds are unconstitutional and otherwise illegal.
2. The issuance of citations, after it has been determined that issuance of a citation is inappropriate, is unconstitutional and otherwise illegal.
3. A practice of allowing a supervisor to override a determination of an officer investigating at the scene is unconstitutional and otherwise illegal, in the absence of facts showing the supervisor had reasonable and probable grounds to cause a citation to issue.
4. Placing known erroneous entries in a citation or crash report to supply a rationale for the citation or conclusions of the crash report is unconstitutional and otherwise illegal.
5. Traffic court use of crash reports to contradict the testimony of witnesses without providing said report to the parties and without appearance and authentication by the police officer is unconstitutional and otherwise illegal.
6. A *de facto* quota system for traffic citations is unconstitutional and otherwise illegal.
7. A system which causes citations to be issued to generate funds for the Police Pension Fund is unconstitutional and otherwise illegal.
8. The practice of reducing employee or city contributions to the pension fund, based upon [auto insurance] premium tax revenues received, is unconstitutional and otherwise illegal.
9. The practice of having insurance companies contribute to the police pension funds, based upon a percentage of premiums collected, is unconstitutional and otherwise illegal.
10. The practice and policy of keeping police officers away from court and not honoring subpoenas is unconstitutional and otherwise illegal.
11. Refusing to give information to citizens that is required to be given, so the citizen can protest citations, is unconstitutional and otherwise illegal.

At the outset, I assumed federal court was a place of ultimate honesty and integrity, where judges make rulings based on laws, facts and with objectivity—*truth, justice and the American way*. My assumptions were entirely wrong. Judge Steven Merryday was eventually assigned to my case. He not only ignored untruthful statements made in court filings by City of Tampa attorneys and officials, he repeated some of their falsities while also ignoring the evidence submitted by my attorney. I later discovered Judge Merryday had presided over five other plaintiff lawsuits against the City of Tampa and each outcome was similar, with the City prevailing.

Of greater concern, Judge Merryday's rulings read as if they were written by attorneys from the automobile insurance industry. He sanctioned the City of Tampa's practices, recognizing auto insurance companies were the primary beneficiary of the tickets—a $1 billion insurance increase in Tampa over 10 years. By sanctioning Tampa's practices, Judge Merryday not only allowed Tampa to continue its practices, but his ruling would allow other law enforcement agencies and courts in the Middle District of Florida to adopt Tampa's policies, which included ticket quotas that result in fraud, a ticket at every rear-end crash due to fault and regardless of probable cause, the secret submission of false crash reports to court to advance convictions, and the kickback from auto insurance companies to "extra" police pension benefits. Judge Merryday did not perceive *any* issue that might violate the U.S. Constitution.

The bottom line? His ruling would allow jurisdictions in the Middle District of Florida to deviate from Florida law to the advantage of auto insurance companies. Rear-end crashes are a common type of accident and tend to be minor. In Florida, minor crashes did not require a police investigation. However, Judge Merryday supported a ticket at every rear-end crash due to *fault* (who pays damages), while simultaneously denying a ticket-at-every-crash policy existed. This was duplicitous. He never mentioned that "fault" was inadmissible in Florida traffic ticket hearings, and he was attempting to shift law (via federal case law) away from ticketing based on probable cause that a traffic violation occurred to ticketing based on who should pay damages, which Ralph Nader's book in 1965 had attributed to proprietary corporate interests. Judge Merryday's rulings reminded me of another lawsuit where insurance companies used a federal lawsuit to create case law to advance their own financial interests.

My familiarity with this other lawsuit began when advising the Florida Attorney General's (AG) Division of Economic Crimes regarding consumer complaints about HMO health insurance plans. Some HMOs were accused of denying payment for needed medical services. The AG attorneys planned to enter into agreements with the offending HMOs, whereby HMOs would agree to abide by certain terms. A point of contention was the definition of medical necessity. HMOs wanted a "cost element" included in the definition, meaning they could choose the lowest cost health care intervention, such as an inexpensive, less effective medication instead of a more costly effective drug. Uniformly applying a cost element is disadvantageous to patients, especially if not required to consider a patient's health status and co-morbid conditions.

Subsequently, several large HMOs used a federal court case in Florida to insert their "medical necessity" definition that included the cost element. A number of state medical associations and large physician groups had filed a federal lawsuit against some large HMOs for not paying them on time. A federal judge in Miami presided over the settlement agreement. While the HMOs inserted their medical necessity definition into the proposed settlement agreement, physicians likely did not oppose the language since it is a consumer (patient) concern, unrelated to physician concerns about being paid on time. Florida's AG attorneys provided a "friend of the court" affidavit to the federal judge and had me do likewise, advising against the cost element in the medical necessity definition. Nonetheless, the HMO cost element was included in the medical necessity definition in the final settlement agreement. The AG attorneys then abandoned their efforts to enter into agreements with the HMOs, since a definition of medical necessity had been created by federal case law and it included the cost element. The Florida AG efforts had been usurped by a single federal judge in Miami.

Apparently, laws of the land can be created by a lone federal judge. It appeared City of Tampa attorneys and Judge Merryday attempted to do likewise. Judge Merryday endorsed Tampa police policies and practices, despite the clear violations of Florida law. Since federal rulings can trump State law, his rulings were a victory for auto insurance companies and policing for profit, at least in the Middle District of Florida.

I looked for potential avenues of influence that might encourage Judge Merryday to advance Tampa's policies and auto insurance interests and found three. Another federal district judge, Susan Bucklew, is a Tampa native and was a local judge prior to her federal appointment. She was copied on Judge Stringer's memo back in 1985, which approved the use of crash reports in lieu of officers appearing in court, making her party to this local practice. As a federal judge, she had the ability to discuss my lawsuit with Judge Merryday. She is now a senior judge and only takes cases of interest to her. A 2014 case involved a lawsuit against the Tampa police, affirming the Tampa Police Department is among her interests.

In addition, Judge Merryday involved Magistrate Judge Mark Pizzo in my federal case who is also a Tampa native. Both the magistrate judge and Judge Bucklew are members of the Herbert G. Goldburg Criminal Law American Inn of Court, which holds mandatory monthly dinner meetings. Inns of Court are clubs, purportedly to advance ethics and professionalism. Members are judges and attorneys, including attorneys who represent corporate interests. At least one member of this Inn of Court is an attorney who represents automobile insurance corporate interests. Consequently, this Inn of Court provides a means to influence federal judges and create bias in favor of auto insurance interests. To answer the question of whether judges give preference in court to "members," the American Inns of Court website stated: "*There is a strong assumption that neither judges nor lawyers will use their Inn membership in a way that would violate their ethical duties."* Meanwhile, I believe corporate interests will do *whatever* to advantage their financial interests, including influencing federal judges via Inns of Court.

A third avenue also existed to influence Judge Merryday. I asked an experienced Tampa police detective to explain how politicians, judges and appointed public officials become corrupt, based on his extensive experience in investigating corruption. Around 2000, when examining a corruption case, the detective had uncovered a video of the local State Attorney in Tampa being "serviced" by a prostitute. The detective explained the video was used by a "lingerie shop" to control the State Attorney, e.g., avoiding prostitution charges. Subsequent to the video being reported in the news, Governor Jeb Bush announced an investigation of the State Attorney over gambling issues.[41] The State Attorney then committed suicide, although I believe he was murdered.

The Tampa detective explained that corrupt interests get well-intentioned public officials to engage in some illegal or shady act, such as taking money or having sex with a prostitute, as the State Attorney had apparently done. It can be anything that, if revealed, would ruin their future as a public official. Corrupt interests only need a well-intentioned public official to do this *once*, since the evidence of even one immoral act allows for manipulating the person forever. If the official does not go along with what they are asked to do, such as "fixing" a court case, the evidence can be used to destroy their political or public career. The method relies on enticing public officials to do something they should not have done, requiring only a single offense. The detective said it is easier to get officials to engage in sex with a prostitute than to take money, which I assume is because the official does not know they are being set-up with a prostitute.

While speculating on why Judge Merryday ruled as he did, only the judge can account for why he repeated falsities made by City of

---

41 The video was not investigated, possibly because the Florida Department of Law Enforcement had difficulty remembering whether or not they received the video—resulting in pondering and equivocating about the video.

Tampa attorneys and ignored essentially all evidence submitted by my attorney. Unfortunately, due to the lax accountability systems that exist in the federal court system, it is doubtful Judge Merryday will be held accountable for his rulings in my case.

After submitting my lawsuit in August 2004, the City of Tampa's external counsel (whose previous career was "police officer") filed a Motion to Dismiss and Motion for Summary Judgment. The motion claimed *"there are no issues of genuine material fact, there were no constitutional violations and therefore there can be no cause of action against the City of Tampa."* It referenced numerous court cases that provided legal nuances. The City's response stated it *"does not have a quota system of any kind"* and *"nothing could be further from the truth."* Affidavits were attached from Police Chief Hogue, Major John Bennett and Officer Duncan (the rookie who wrote my crash report) that stated a traffic ticket quota did not exist. The police chief's affidavit stated the police department does not have *"any plan or scheme that intentionally and/or artificially attempts to increase the issuance of Uniform Traffic Citations"* and that citations are issued *"at the discretion"* of individual officers.

The City's motion contended Judge Stringer's 1985 memorandum allows them to submit crash reports to court in lieu of the officer's appearance, making no reference to the Florida law that bans the use of crash reports in court, or that the reports are never entered into the court record. The City's motion stated that my claiming John Bennett did not respond to my numerous complaints is *"baseless,"* and that the court has found citizens do not have a right to an Internal Affairs investigation, recognizing I had evidence of a felony. Bennett was untruthful in his affidavit, since he wrote, *"Further, at no time did I nor could I direct former Mayor Dick Greco to answer or not answer any letter from citizens, including by* [sic] *not limited to those of Dr. Orban."*

However, an e-mail affirmed he did so. Bennett had sent an e-mail to the Mayor's Executive Aide, advising that it was unnecessary to respond to my complaint. The content of his e-mail is evidence he was untruthful in his affidavit, yet he was not fired for untruthfulness or prosecuted for perjury.[42]

The City's motion concluded that I received my "substantive and procedural due process rights," making no mention that their false crash report resulted in a nearly $4,000 auto insurance increase that helped fund "extra" Tampa police pension benefits or that I could have received a refund from my insurance company had they merely corrected the crash report errors.

The affidavit of Officer Bowden (who wrote my careless driving ticket) stated the basis for the ticket was that I "skidded" into the rear of the other car and "*was therefore at fault.*" He made no mention of a driving violation. However, who paid damages (fault) is inadmissible in Florida traffic courts, meaning he would need another rationale for the ticket if testifying at the traffic court hearing. The officer wrote that he may have advised me that "*Tampa Officers are generally required to issue traffic citations to the party at fault in traffic accidents which are investigated by the CITY OF TAMPA Police Department.*" This is what I was alleging—he used the word *REQUIRED* and *FAULT*, which affirmed the Tampa Police Department required officers to write tickets in 100% of accidents, regardless of the officer's conclusion about probable cause that a traffic infraction occurred. Further, the police do not determine who is at-fault, since insurance companies do this and any disputes are settled in jury trials. For example, a Florida legislator rear-ended a truck and received a ticket. He subsequently sued the company that owned the truck. In 2010, a jury awarded him more than $800,000 for his injuries, meaning he received a ticket from an officer, but fault was attributed to the truck driver.

---

42 The content of Bennett's email is as follows: "*She wrote us several months ago—I addressed everything in her letter (very detailed) and responded. She was not happy and wrote another letter, micro-assessing my letter. I filed it with no response. I then found out she called internal affairs and started the whole process all over again. They dealt with her for a while and took my letter and kept a file. I received the letter she sent to the Mayor, and planned to file it with the others. There really is no need to respond anymore to her concerns, as she is simply shopping for her answer. She ammends [sic] her story evertime [sic] to solicit more action. I outlined everything she could/should do in the first letter, and even let our legal advisor read it for verification (he agreed).*"

Police officers only assess whether a traffic law was violated. This was affirmed when the Tampa police changed their policy around the time the appellate court was reviewing my appeal of Judge Merryday's rulings. The Tampa Police Department announced that insurance companies, and not the police, determine fault and they discontinued writing tickets in minor non-injury crashes. Officer Bowden subsequently told me that officers were re-trained and that if my accident occurred now, he would be prohibited from writing a ticket or a long-form crash report. This affirms Judge Merryday's ruling was incorrect, which contended tickets are issued based on *fault*, instead of a traffic violation.

Having the unique experience of being a plaintiff in a federal lawsuit, I discovered it was about as exciting as watching paint dry or grass grow. It was painfully slow-moving and dragged on for nearly four years. Yet, I never once had an opportunity to say a single word in front of a judge, much less a jury. When it was over, I concluded that federal court was the most dishonest and unprofessional operation imaginable. My experience is best characterized as "pathologic lying" among Tampa's attorneys and the federal judges involved. This likely occurred due to the lack of accountability systems. When public officials, including federal judges, do not encounter any consequences for being untruthful, they can fabricate whatever they choose. Pathologic lying occurs when individuals lose their ability to differentiate truth from fiction, which is encouraged in a justice system that does not hold officials accountable for whether or not they tell the truth. There are relatively straightforward means to prevent this and improve accountability. While imperfect, they are better than nothing, as currently exists in the justice system. It was disturbing that Judge Merryday could send people to prison and yet no oversight exists regarding his honesty and integrity.

I always knew I could lose, but not in the way a federal district judge, magistrate judge, and three appellate court judges permitted—fraught with substantial omissions of facts, along with some falsities, which is what I was accusing the Tampa police of doing.

The sluggish ordeal entailed motions being sent back and forth to court, and then again and again, from my attorney and the City's attorneys. At first, I thought this was good. Both sides document facts for the judge's review, but I eventually learned otherwise. The City of Tampa's untruthfulness and misrepresentations simply extended into their motions and affidavits, which Judge Merryday ignored or repeated. The judge unabashedly blocked my case from proceeding to a jury trial by engaging in his own omissions and fabrications.

Once learning Judge Merryday was presiding over my case, I had immediate concerns, due to his management of another plaintiff's case, which was dismissed shortly before I filed my lawsuit. I feared Judge Merryday's management of the other plaintiff's case against a law enforcement official would provide a crystal ball into how he would manage my case. It did.

The plaintiff in the other case was Assistant U.S. Attorney Jeffrey Del Fuoco who worked in the public corruption unit. Prior to filing his lawsuit, Mr. Del Fuoco had successfully prosecuted a squad of Manatee County sheriff's deputies who were found guilty of planting evidence, stealing cash from drug dealers, giving crack cocaine to informants, and lying on search warrants and reports. About 100 convictions were overturned as a consequence of this federal case, which is the upshot of investigating dishonest law enforcement officers.

In his plaintiff's case, Mr. Del Fuoco sued the sheriff of Manatee County, Charlie Wells, along with a few of the sheriff's employees. Mr. Del Fuoco alleged the sheriff retaliated against him shortly after the convictions of his deputies by accessing his personal information, which occurred after Mr. Del Fuoco announced his investigation of the sheriff's office was ongoing. Mr. Del Fuoco found a sheriff's employee used the tag numbers from his vehicle to obtain personal information from the Florida Crime Information Center, including his home address. The employee, who accessed this data, said the request came from the same narcotics unit that Mr. Del Fuoco had prosecuted. Del Fuoco's lawsuit alleged illegal access of law enforcement data to "harm, injure and harass" his family and him. He also alleged being stalked and that his house was being staked out.

Prior to filing his lawsuit, Mr. Del Fuoco had asked the U.S. Attorney of the Middle District of Florida (Paul Perez) for protection, as he feared for the safety of himself and his family. Mr. Del Fuoco claimed Mr. Perez and the U.S. Department of Justice offered nothing for the security of himself or his family at the time he was investigating the sheriff, so he filed his lawsuit against the sheriff and the employee who accessed his personal information, later adding others to the lawsuit. Sheriff Wells later claimed Del Fuoco behaved inappropriately by "outing" the undercover vehicle used in the alleged stake-out of the Del Fuoco home.

In July 2003, Judge Merryday denied a motion to dismiss the Del Fuoco lawsuit, allowing the case to proceed. A year later, Judge Merryday dismissed the case over a period of months, the dismissal of each person handled separately. It appeared the judge planned to dismiss it all along, but allowed further expense to occur on the part of the plaintiff to teach him a lesson about the hazards of daring to set foot into federal court.[43] In the end, Del Fuoco resigned and the sheriff did not seek re-election. A federal judge ordered Mr. Del Fuoco to reimburse the sheriff $167,000 for his legal expenses.

This outcome concerned me. I asked Mr. Magri if Judge Merryday could do this to me—string my case along for years, allowing more and more expense to occur, and then dismiss it piece by piece—preventing a jury from hearing the facts and then ordering me to pay the City's legal expenses. He said it was possible, but unlikely I would be required to reimburse the City for its legal expenses. Judge Merryday ultimately toyed with my case for several years, allowing more and more expense to accrue to me in court filings, and then he dismissed it piece by piece, just as in Mr. Del Fuoco's case. However, the appellate court required me to reimburse the City of Tampa only $80.

Personally, I had a very high opinion of Mr. Del Fuoco. Among all the people in all the agencies to which I made a complaint about

---

43 Prior to filing my lawsuit, my attorney warned me that federal judges tend to be disapproving of plaintiff cases, perhaps because it provides additional work for them.

Tampa police policies, Mr. Del Fuoco was the *only* person who agreed to investigate my complaint. After I explained Tampa's practices to him, he said he had concerns about them and asked me to send the related documents. Within a week or so, he was moved out of the public corruption unit—thereby no longer able to investigate my complaint. I called the public corruption unit a few more times, but no one responded after Mr. Del Fuoco was transferred from it. Later, the U.S. Attorney Paul Perez resigned to become a corporate insurance executive, and Mr. Del Fuoco's supervisor in the public corruption unit, who helped force his resignation (Robert O'Neill), eventually became the U.S. Attorney for the Middle District of Florida.

Judge Merryday ignored my lawsuit for about a year. Then, he created additional expense for me by having my attorney rewrite the complaint, changing it from a 2-count to a 4-count complaint. This ultimately gave him more counts to dismiss over time, thereby creating more expense for me.

At the first of only two hearings that occurred in my case, reporters from both the *St. Petersburg Times* and *Tampa Tribune* attended. My allegations of ticket quotas and the kickback arrangement between insurers and police pension benefits became public knowledge. My attorney and I received numerous telephone calls. My attorney received calls from a few Tampa police officers who offered to help. One officer explained he writes "per supervisor" on tickets ordered by the supervisor when believing probable cause did not exist to issue a ticket in a crash investigation. Mr. Magri took the officers' names and contact information. Meanwhile, I received telephone calls and letters from people with concerns about their own experiences with Tampa police ticketing fraud. They were potential additional witnesses if my case progressed to a jury trial.

In court filings, attorneys for the City of Tampa claimed I had no proof of the alleged Tampa police policy to write a ticket at every crash investigation. They ignored the fact that Officer Bowden's annual evaluation in 2000 revealed the number of crashes he investigated precisely equaled the number of tickets he issued in crash investigations. Further, a retired Tampa sergeant provided an affidavit that explained the ticket-at-every-crash policy, as well as Tampa's ticket quota for patrol officers. In addition, the sergeant documented it would be impossible for a judge to differentiate a ticket that was written based on probable cause in a crash investigation from one ordered by the supervisor.[44]

The sergeant's affidavit was reported in the *Tampa Tribune*, precipitating something most beneficial. A few days after the news article appeared, a Tampa police lieutenant distributed the ticket and arrest quotas in writing at roll call.[45] I had the document within a

---

44 An excerpt from the retired sergeant's affidavit is as follows: *"The training at the Tampa Police Department's Field Training and Evaluation Program (FTEP) in recent years instructed new recruits that they must write a traffic citation every time an officer investigates a crash. FTEP taught recruits that discretion does not exist in whether or not to write a traffic citation as traffic citations are always required as part of crash investigations. I am aware of this teaching, since I have had approximately five or six new recruits under my supervision in recent years and all have explained this FTEP policy to me.*

*If a supervisor requires a citation, consistent with the FTEP training, then the officer is forced to write a citation and record the violation as the contributing cause on the crash report, despite the officer's inability to conclude a traffic law violation occurred... It would not be possible to differentiate a citation and crash report that an officer wrote based on objective conclusions from a personal investigation from a citation and crash report ordered by a supervisor.*

*In 2003, I had two new recruits begin under my supervision. Both initially asked for my verbal concurrence that they will write traffic citations at every crash investigation, consistent with the FTEP training. I asked them what they would tell a judge when subpoenaed to a traffic hearing over a citation for which reasonable evidence did not exist to conclude a traffic law violation occurred. Both recruits responded that this would not be a problem, because they would not testify in front of a judge. Instead of appearing in person, they explained they would send the crash report and therefore would not be required to testify before a judge about the citation. Both claimed their FTEP training instructed them that personal testimony would not be required regarding such violations.*

*I retrained all five or six recruits who were assigned to me in recent years, since a citation cannot be written unless the officer has reasonable and objective information that a traffic law violation occurred. In the absence of such, a citation cannot be written. As a supervisor, I approved all requests by my officers to not write a citation. The patrol officer personally conducts a crash investigation and has facts on whether a traffic law was or was not violated.*

45 This was the email correspondence provided in Chapter 3.

few hours. Apparently, the lieutenant enforced the quota, but did not approve of it. My attorney submitted it to the court as further evidence of the ticket quotas.

The City's court filings also contended the memo from Judge Stringer was a "fact." The memo is a "fact," but the practice Judge Stringer approved violated Florida law. The City also claimed I had no proof that every accident is reported to the insurance company, so my attorney hired an auto insurance expert who would explain the industry's practices in order to refute the City's contention.

Mr. Magri took the depositions of Officers Bowden and Duncan, and told me Officer Bowden's deposition was very helpful. Officer Bowden had clear recall of his investigation of my minor accident, which had occurred more than five years prior to his deposition and despite his investigating 4,000 crashes over 19 years. The officer said the following about me: "*She's a pleasant lady.*" Mr. Magri explained this favorable comment would be important to a jury as it sets a tone for our discussion. Officer Bowden reported the accident damage was "*fairly minimal.*" He said it was sprinkling or had just rained, the parking lot surface was wet, and added the following about the traffic ticket: "*I don't recall if it was following too closely or careless driving. As I recall, her vehicle struck the back of the other involved vehicle in the rear, and that would have been the choice of the two options, at the time, for the citation.*"

Officer Bowden affirmed Tampa's policy required a ticket and crash report at minor crashes. He explained he was part of a Field Training squad, training a new police officer when investigating my accident. Mr. Margi asked the question, "*Do you have any specific recollection that you had it in your mind that you were not going to give Dr. Orban a ticket based on the accident information?*" Officer Bowden then revealed how he had avoided writing tickets in crash investigations. When electing to not issue a ticket, he did not write a crash report, such that a discrepancy did not exist between the number of crashes investigated and the number of tickets issued in crash investigations. With my accident, he explained that he was training a new officer; therefore, this was not an option.[46] He explained the "documentation" (ticket and 4-page crash report) was for the benefit of the insurance company and he perceived it as unrelated to police work. He said there was a time when the Tampa police did not respond to accidents with no injuries, if vehicles were drivable; but this changed, and now they respond to every crash, regardless of how minor.

Officer Bowden acknowledged that Careless Driving may not have been an appropriate charge, relative to my accident. He explained that he expected my ticket to be dismissed in court, because no one would attend to testify against me.

When asked about the traffic ticket expectations, unrelated to crashes, he responded that there is a "recommended number" and admitted a large increase in traffic tickets had occurred.

He receives "below expectation" ratings in traffic law enforcement, because his tickets are less than the district average. He had a "below expectation" rating for many years and explained his low number of traffic tickets is because he focuses on responding to calls for service.[47] He rated himself in the top 1% of officers in responding to calls for police service. Nonetheless, the goal given to him in annual evaluations was to improve his traffic law enforcement—write

---

46 Officer Bowden explained this as follows:

"I can't recall at that time in my career if I was doing the exchanges [Exchange of Information form], even though that was maybe not what was expected in a minimal crash like this. But because I was training, sometimes that affects a little bit of your procedures, as far as I can't go out and just, 'Do as I say and not as I do.' So you have to lead by example. So we were dispatched to a crash. The procedures generally followed are that if you get dispatched to the crash, you investigate and issue a citation. That's the only thing I can—like I said, just a general recollection that—I don't know if I might have relayed that to her that, "Look, I'm training and we're going to go ahead and do the crash because we're here."

47 Officer Bowden stated the following:

"My time or my perspective on police work in patrol is, I'm there to respond to the public, as far as calls that come in, and I don't put much weight on traffic law enforcement. If there's a good observed violation that occurs in front of me, you know, I would stop that individual and deal with that situation. I'm radar-certified. I haven't run radar, I don't think, in numerous years. I just don't put the weight on that and I 'm able to occupy my time at work by just responding to calls for service."

more traffic tickets. He said he prefers recommending roadway engineering improvements to improve traffic safety.

In contrast, when Officer Duncan (the trainee who wrote my crash report) was deposed, he claimed to not recall the accident or investigation, which contradicted his affidavit. Nonetheless, he expected my ticket to be dismissed in court because it did not identify a careless driving action. Since both officers believed the ticket would be dismissed, as stated in their depositions, it is not credible that probable cause existed to write a ticket.

Police Chief Hogue was also deposed. Mr. Magri asked if accidents can occur that are unavoidable. The chief responded, *"Absolutely true that once an accident series starts, some things that happen are unavoidable."* The police chief said mistakes made on crash reports should be corrected and any phantom vehicle should be included in the crash report diagram if it fits the circumstances. It becomes clear the police chief's views differ from Tampa police attorneys Rainsberger and Richardson, who refused to correct the report.

Police Chief Hogue further explained that a driver should receive a ticket in rear-end accident circumstances, even when using a correct following distance, because the driver is "culpable in the accident." He defines culpable as *"did something that violated the traffic statutes to cause that accident or to contribute to the causation of that accident."* It was contradictory, as the police chief believes some accidents are unavoidable, yet all entail a violation of a traffic law. The police chief explained his perspective as follows: *"A traffic citation for $150 or $200, you're taking food out of their kids' mouths, and their rent's got to be paid and their house payment has got to be paid... But on the same token, it is their job to write traffic citations, enforce the traffic laws... But police officers as a general rule do not enjoy writing traffic tickets."*

Chief Hogue's statement was Scrooge-like, demanding tickets that interfere with paying the rent or feeding the kids, while he personally profited from tickets via a gigantic pension increase. With regard to the insurance money that accrues to the police pension, Police Chief Hogue said he believed the police department was paid by insurance companies to investigate crashes, that is, until I came along. After reading this, I thought, *How could I lose?* Officer Bowden and the police chief both believed they were investigating crashes for auto insurance companies.

The police chief denied the existence of a quota system and said, "*It's illegal.*" He went on to say traffic enforcement is part of the job, adding, "*If they don't do their job, then, yes, they probably are rated below expectations or unsatisfactory.*" This was contradictory and affirms quotas are called "expectations" to avoid the appearance of an illegal activity.

Mr. Magri recommended that to win in court, an expert should reconstruct my accident to demonstrate to a jury how it occurred. He identified an expert who met the *Daubert* standard, which is required of experts in federal court to affirm the person has scientific knowledge on the subject. It precludes "junk scientists" from feigning as experts. We met with the reconstruction expert who stated he is a "scientist" and would report only what he found.

My rate of speed when rear-ending the other car could be determined from the receipt from my car repair, which specified the repairs made. I gave the weather documentation to him, which included satellite data purchased from the National Oceanic and Atmospheric Administration (NOAA) and the documentation that affirmed it was the first rain in many months. The 4-page crash report identified the location of the crash, which was just beyond the intersection. The expert took my statements regarding my rate of speed and following distance behind the SUV. He then went to the intersection and took relevant measurements and pictures. My automobile manufacturer provided him with information specific to my car and braking system. He had everything needed to estimate my rate of speed on impact, based on the damage, to compare with the rate expected, based on my description of circumstances, as well as affirm my following distance.

I had been driving at 15 mph, following a large SUV that, without signaling, turned off the road directly in front of stopped traffic. My reported following distance exceeded the distance the Tampa police training officers said should be used. In our final meeting, the expert let me know everything fit and he explained why the crash was unavoidable. He created a graphic that illustrated when I would first be able to see stopped traffic. Until then, my car was moving forward at 15 mph (22 feet per second), which continued during the perception/reaction time to braking. He provided research that explained in unexpected situations, the perception/reaction time is slightly longer than the 1-second average. My automobile manufacturer provided the length of delay for the anti-lock brakes to engage in the wet road conditions, during which time my car was still moving forward at 22 feet per second. Thus, the gap to the stopped traffic was being closed during the delay in being able to view stopped traffic, the perception/reaction time to braking, and the delay in the anti-lock brakes engaging. He said it was only seconds between the time the SUV began turning and my bumping into the stopped car that I could not see. Further, he said wet road conditions made the stopping distance unpredictable due to road-oil conditions, which are not uniform. He explained how rain, especially the first rain after a dry period, leads to variability in the distance needed to stop. The expert also stated that because the SUV turned instead of stopped, I was deprived of the distance it would take the SUV to stop.[48] He would testify that my accident was unavoidable.

Mr. Magri submitted the expert's affidavit and analysis to court. The City's counsel responded that it was biased, but made no attempt to create an alternative analysis of accident circumstances. Though they employ officers who reconstruct accidents, they never refuted the expert's analysis using facts. For no discernible reason, their "strategy" worked. Judge Merryday ignored the expert's analysis. So much for science in federal court.

Judge Merryday ordered mediation, which turned out to be another tactic to make me spend more money. The judge should know the City of Tampa would never mediate, as I had been asking them

---

48 When stopping, drivers typically have their following distance plus the distance it takes the forward vehicle to stop.

to reconsider their policies for the past five years. Mediation occurred in November 2005. What I wanted from mediation was very clear, as stated in the declarations made in my legal complaint. I wanted the Tampa police to amend their policies to conform with State law. Florida had reasonable laws, just no means of enforcing them. My specific settlement requests, made in writing for mediation, can be disclosed because the City of Tampa attorneys were untruthful about what I sought (See Appendix B).

The mediator and the attorneys exited the room and I was left sitting with the police representative, Assistant Police Chief Jane Castor, who later became Tampa's police chief in 2009. Since this was not part of the mediation, I can repeat what she said. She confided that if they were unsuccessful with their motions to dismiss and for summary judgment, they would settle with me. She explained they would *"never let this go to a jury trial."* To me, this was an admission of intentional wrongdoing. However, her first choice was to have a judge allow them to continue their self-serving practices. The mediation outcome was that it would be "continued."

My case was scheduled for a jury trial in July 2006, but first Judge Merryday would rule on the City's motions to dismiss and for summary judgment. Based on the affidavits, depositions, and documentation of the quota, I did not believe a jury trial could be denied. However, I never got my day in court, because this, I came to recognize, was federal kangaroo court.

# CHAPTER 10

# CASE FIXING

## Why You Can't Beat City Hall

*"...the City employs no policy that requires issuance of a citation."*
Federal District Judge Steven D. Merryday
July 31, 2006

On April 4, 2006, Judge Merryday issued an order on Count 1, ruling that waiting for the officers to fabricate a ticket and crash report in a police investigation that was not required by law did not impose *"the slightest deprivation of liberty."* He dismissed Count 1. However, I never cared about the Count 1 detention issue, even though Florida law required contacting the police for any accident that entailed $500 or more in damages. Nonetheless, it was disturbing that Judge Merryday repeated the City's allegation that I was "initially adjudged guilty," since it was untrue. It signaled the judge was either inattentive to facts or willing to repeat false statements made by the City's attorneys, especially as my attorney had pointed out this statement was untrue after the City made the claim. Judge Merryday had the court record to reference that affirmed his statement was untrue, yet he parroted attorneys for the City of Tampa.

The City entered motions to dismiss Counts 2 and 3 (malicious prosecution), as well as motions for "summary judgment" on these counts, while also moving for "summary judgment" on Count 4—the due process violations.[49] Judge Merryday could only grant summary judgment if both sides agree on the facts. In contrast, a motion to dismiss could be granted if the judge concluded my lawsuit should not be allowed to proceed due to some legal deficiency. The judge denied without prejudice the City's motion for summary judgment on Count 4. He explained that one must demonstrate a constitutional violation and that it occurred as a result of the "initiation of a prosecution," which would require more submissions from Mr. Magri to demonstrate a constitutional violation (meaning more expense for me).

The judge denied the City's motion to dismiss Counts 2 and 3 without prejudice, each of which alleged malicious prosecution, and instead would rule on whether probable cause existed for the ticket. Probable cause is defined as "a reasonable belief that a person has committed a crime." It is a relatively low standard, based on suspicion alone. For a malicious prosecution case to move forward, the citation had to be issued without probable cause. The judge ordered that discovery should continue on whether probable cause existed for the ticket. If probable cause existed, he would rule in favor of the City on Counts 2 and 3.

Regarding summary judgment, Mr. Magri told me the judge is not permitted to make credibility determinations. Only a jury can make credibility determinations. Mr. Magri said we did not agree on the facts, a required condition for Judge Merryday to grant summary judgment. In my deposition and affidavit, I explained that Officer Bowden told me I did not violate a traffic law. The City does not agree with this, meaning we do not agree. Mr. Magri informed me the judge is not allowed to rule in favor of the City by choosing *not* to believe me, as only juries are allowed to make credibility determinations. He said the City will file their motion for summary judgment, and he will respond that we do not agree on the facts, thereby leading to a jury trial.

---

49 The American Bar Association defines "due process" as follows:
*The concept that laws and legal proceedings must be fair. The Constitution guarantees that the government cannot take away a person's basic rights to life, liberty or property, without due process of law. Courts have issued numerous rulings about what this means in particular cases.*

However, I thought sufficient information existed for me to be granted summary judgment. A driving violation had never been identified, and the City claims to write tickets to the trailing car in all rear-end collisions, regardless of the findings of an investigation. The police chief said he believed the Tampa police were paid to investigate crashes for insurance companies, hence explaining why they must identify and ticket an *at fault* driver. Officer Bowden expressed he likely would not have written a ticket, if not training a new officer in Tampa's ticket-at-every-crash policy. Further, he explained that if dispatched to a crash, he was expected to write a ticket and report. In depositions, both Officers Duncan and Bowden said they expected my ticket to be dismissed, which is contrary to believing probable cause existed. These are facts that can be agreed upon, because they exist in depositions and affidavits. This seemed sufficient evidence that there is no issue of material fact to be tried. The City's attorneys believe a ticket should be issued to the rear driver regardless of an investigation's findings, and both the police chief and Officer Bowden explained this is done for the insurance company.

I asked Mr. Magri to file a motion for summary judgment on my behalf. His final product was very comprehensive and referenced more than 20 legal cases. It declared the City argues that the Careless Driving statute fails to identify items such as a car's speed or how far one is following another, suggesting those facts are not material to careless driving; whereas Florida's statute does, in fact, stipulate "attendant circumstances" are material. It noted if a careless driving action cannot be specified, then there cannot be probable cause for careless driving, referencing the Florida court decision that requires officers to list the specific elements of the careless driving charge on the traffic citation. The omission corroborates that Officer Bowden did not find a careless driving action. The motion asserted that my explanation of circumstances cannot be ignored.[50] It noted the City's posture to ignore statements made by Officer Bowden in his deposition. The

---

50 With regard to the false crash report, Mr. Magri cited the ruling from the *Kingsland v. City of Miami* case, which found it is an *"error for the district court to omit the plaintiff's allegations of falsification and knowing lack of probable cause from its analysis."*

motion stated Officer Bowden *never* testified in his deposition or affidavit that he believed probable cause existed to write a ticket.

Not surprisingly, the City responded with matching affidavits from Officers Bowden and Duncan that perfunctorily state, "*I reasonably believed that there was probable cause for the issuance*" of a careless driving ticket. This was remarkable to me, since a year earlier, Officer Duncan could not recall the accident investigation during his deposition. Officer Bowden's affidavit about probable cause contradicted his deposition. The affidavits are evidence that City of Tampa attorneys can get officers to sign anything. In both affidavits, the explanation for issuing a ticket to me was that they did not find a reason to ticket the other driver, which affirms the expectation for a ticket-at-every-crash and that City of Tampa attorneys were using my lawsuit to sanction their ticket-at-every-crash policy.

In addition to my motion for summary judgment, Mr. Magri also responded to the City's motion for summary judgment, which was submitted by Tampa City Attorney, David L. Smith, and Assistant City Attorney, Ursula Richardson. As in past submissions, their entire argument stated I was *at fault* and hence cited for careless driving. They used Florida's *rear-end presumption* law to justify the ticket, which holds rear drivers responsible for paying for damages in a rear-end crash, absent mitigating circumstances.

Mr. Smith and Ms. Richardson wrote, "*Although a sudden stop is a recognized exception, no exception has necessarily been carved out for a 'sudden turn;' however, the premise of a sudden turn to rebut the presumption is comparable to the premise of a sudden stop,*" referencing *Clampitt v. D.J. Spencer Sales*, which was a lawsuit about who should pay for damages. They concluded an abrupt turn is comparable to an abrupt stop in rebutting fault for a rear-end accident, which supports not issuing a ticket, making it unclear why they wrote this.

The City attorneys wrote, "*The Plaintiff was 'at fault' and deserving of the traffic citation she received in this case, and therefore summary judgment for the City is appropriate.*" They identified seven *facts* that were known to the officers and precipitated the ticket, none of which pertained to an improper driving action, only that a rear-end accident occurred.[51] The City Attorney took the position that any rear-end accident, regardless of circumstances, constitutes careless driving, further explaining, *"The fact that the Plaintiff offered a justification for **why** she rear-ended ... does not negate the fact that she did 'bump' a stopped car."* Tampa's attorneys were attempting to create federal case law to advantage auto insurance companies, whereby all rear-end crashes are *de facto* careless driving. They believed *why* an accident occurred is irrelevant, which is even contrary to Florida's *rear-end presumption* law. This occurred at the same time proprietary interests were promoting legalizing red-light cameras in Florida, which are cameras that *increase* rear-end crashes by 50-60%.

The City Attorney wrote, *"Had the Plaintiff been **more careful**, she would likely have been able to adjust her driving to compensate for any abrupt or sudden change in the traffic patterns of that day and avoid hitting"* the other vehicle. Their definition of "careless" had morphed from driving in a careless manner to whether it was possible to be *more careful*. This means a driver who is careful, but could have been *more careful*, is hence careless—per Tampa City Attorney David L. Smith and Ursula Richardson, thereby allowing for a ticket at every crash, since it is always possible to be *more careful*.

Mr. Magri's response to the City's motion for summary judgment stated that failing to consider the foregoing facts of an investigation is a violation of the City's duty to consider the facts before them.

On July 31, 2006, Judge Merryday denied my motion for summary judgment on Counts 2 and 3 (malicious prosecution) and granted the City's motion for summary judgment on Counts 2 and 3. On page

---

51 The City Attorney's seven "facts" are as follows:
1. *Two cars were involved in a collision;*
2. *Barbara Orban was driving the car that struck the rear of the vehicle;*
3. *The Plaintiff (Orban) agreed that the other car was at a complete stop at the time of this rear-end collision;*
4. *There was visible damage to the rear of M.C.'s car;*
5. *There was visible damage to the front end of the Plaintiff's car;*
6. *Plaintiff admitted that she ran into the back of M.C.'s car; and,*
7. *There were no identifiable independent witnesses to the collision.*

1, in a footnote, he wrote, *"...the City employs no policy that requires issuance of a citation."* This statement is false. Judge Merryday ignored facts, thereby prohibiting a jury trial regarding Tampa's policies.

Judge Merryday also wrote, *"The City employs a policy that requires consultation with a supervisor."* This is untrue. In such circumstances, it is not "consultation" that is sought, but "approval" from the supervisor to *not* issue a ticket. Tampa's policy violates Florida law, which requires a "personal investigation" to issue a ticket in crash investigations, something supervisors do not complete. The judge further wrote that Tampa's policy to contact supervisors is *"the most reasonable policy, or, at the very least, not an unconstitutional policy."* It is unreasonable due to the supervisor's failure to conduct an investigation.

On the topic of probable cause, Judge Merryday cited from another court ruling on probable cause about the investigating officer's knowledge of the facts,[52] which contradicted his earlier statement that requiring the supervisor's approval to not issue a ticket is *"most reasonable."* The investigating officer possesses the "reasonably trustworthy information" to make a decision, not the supervisor. Supervisors are *not* credible decision makers, because they do *not* know the "facts and circumstances." Reading Judge Merryday's ruling reminded me of grading really, really bad papers in college classes I have taught.

Judge Merryday wrote that an officer has probable cause, *"so long as the totality of the circumstances present a sufficient basis for believing that an offense has been committed."* In his deposition, Officer Bowden acknowledged careless driving may not be an appropriate charge and my ticket failed to identify a careless driving action, so the standard identified by Judge Merryday was *not* met.

In his prior ruling on Count 1, Judge Merryday wrote, *"Pursuant to Florida law, the uniform traffic citation constitutes the charging document and initiates prosecution of the traffic violation."* However, in a footnote on his Counts 2 and 3 ruling, Judge Merryday wrote that in most crashes someone is *at fault.* Thus, he correctly understood

---

52 Judge Merryday wrote: *Probable cause "exists where the facts and circumstances within [the officer's] knowledge and of which [the officer] had reasonably trustworthy information (are) sufficient in themselves to warrant a man of reasonable caution in the belief that an offense has been committed or is being committed."*

citations are issued for traffic violations, but was now attempting to create federal case law that allows *fault* to become a legal basis for issuing a ticket in the Middle District of Florida.

Judge Merryday also wrote: *Orban argues that no reasonable person hearing her description of the accident could conclude that she deserved a careless driving citation. However, both officers testify that they relied on the Florida rebuttable presumption that the following driver in a rear-end collision is at fault. Clampitt v. D.J. Spencer Sales (Fla. 2001).*

Judge Merryday's statement above is untrue. The judge had both my affidavit and deposition, so he knew I never said this. Instead, I said Officer Bowden told me I did not violate a traffic law, but his supervisor ordered a ticket nonetheless—meaning Judge Merryday was untruthful about what I said. Further, the *Clampitt* case pertained to who would pay damages and not whether a traffic violation occurred. The court case occurred 14 months after my accident, so it is not credible the officers relied on it in their decision making.

The *Clampitt* case scenario was entirely inapplicable to my situation, other than the context used by the City attorneys, in likening a sudden stop to a sudden turn. The case was a civil lawsuit involving sequential rear-end crashes among vehicles trailing one another, having nothing to do with a traffic ticket.[53]

---

53 In the *Clampitt* case, the Florida Supreme Court ruling explained three vehicles were involved, all initially traveling at 45 to 50 mph. The lead vehicle was a pick-up truck hauling a trailer. It signaled a right turn, slowed, and nearly completed the turn, when Clampitt's car did not stop in time and hit the trailer, resulting in minor damage. Clampitt's car was then rear-ended by a commercial tractor-trailer rig, resulting in major damage. Clampitt filed lawsuits against both the pick-up driver and the tractor-trailer company. There is no mention of Clampitt being ticketed after causing minor damage in a rear-end crash, which Judge Merryday forgot to mention. The lawsuit against the pick-up driver was dismissed, while the tractor-trailer company was ordered to pay $842,997 in damages in a summary judgment ruling as the trailing driver, consistent with Florida's rebuttable presumption law. The decision against the tractor-trailer company was reversed by an appellate court, as the driver of the commercial rig claimed mitigating circumstances, such that a jury would decide who would pay damages. However, the Florida Supreme Court held the tractor-trailer company was liable for the damages, as the commercial rig driver controlled his stopping distance as the trailing driver and had a clear view of the traffic in front of him at all times. He was responsible for damages, due to Florida's law that the trailing driver in a rear-end collision is *at fault* absent mitigating circumstances.

Based on the *Clampitt* case, Judge Merryday wrote:

*Orban's rear-ending the car in front of the leading SUV provides sufficient evidence that Orban failed to push ahead of [herself] an imaginary clear stopping distance. One supposes that a driver's rear-ending the car in front of the car in front of the driver creates an even stronger presumption of the driver's carelessness than the driver's rear-ending the car immediately in front of the driver.*

The "imaginary clear stopping distance" in *Clampitt* pertained to a commercial rig that could see the two vehicles in front of him, circumstances inapplicable to me. It is impossible to have an "imaginary clear stopping distance" for something one cannot see, as the larger vehicle was between me and the car I bumped into. Also, Judge Merryday failed to mention the <u>*Clampitt*</u> case provided content favorable to my case. It states the law assumes the rear driver is negligent, for purposes of paying damages; but this can "*vanish*" if a reasonable explanation is provided. This discredits Tampa's ticket-at-every-crash policy. The law recognizes that some rear-end circumstances may not entail negligence, which is why it is necessary to consider the attendant circumstances.

Judge Merryday cited the following: "*For probable cause to exist… an arrest must be objectively reasonable, based on the totality of the circumstances.*" He wrote the following declaratory statement: "*Finding probable cause, the officers issued Orban a citation for careless driving.*" Officer Bowden did consider the "totality of circumstances" and told me there was no traffic law violation, as evidenced by his failure to document a careless driving action on the ticket, which Judge Merryday ignored. Further, Officer Bowden suggested I file a lawsuit over Tampa's practices. Judge Merryday was not supposed to disregard my statements or those of Officer Bowden, but he did so nonetheless.

Judge Merryday concluded, "*Florida law assumes that every driver can stop her car within that space that she can see (the 'imaginary clear stopping distance').*" He is wrong, since adhering to following distance guides does not consistently provide for an adequate stopping distance, which is why the "presumption" of fault is rebuttable. Further, the expert in the reconstruction of my case explained the math involved in stopping, which Judge Merryday ignored. More importantly, the law did not require a police investigation of my minor crash.

From my perspective, Judge Merryday did something exceedingly sinister. He created federal case law that would allow jurisdictions in the Middle District of Florida to ticket all rear-end crashes for careless driving regardless of circumstances, based on *fault*, which occurred at the same time "special interests" were peddling red-light cameras that increase rear-end crashes. Judge Merryday's ruling was a gift to auto insurance companies, as his newfound federal court rationale for ticketing all rear-end crashes would result in very large auto insurance increases. My lawsuit illustrates how a single federal judge can establish federal case law that advantages corporate interests, absent any oversight. Federal court cases provide a means for corporate interests to trump state laws.

In addition to granting summary judgment in favor of the City on Counts 2 and 3 (Malicious Prosecution), Judge Merryday proceeded to address Count 4, which pertained to violations of due process of law. He concluded that my complaint failed to specify the following: 1) a specific constitutional injury; 2) a violation by the City of Orban's due process rights; 3) a sufficient causal connection between a practice of the City and any constitutional injury to Orban; and 4) an available and effective remedy to redress any constitutional injury. He gave my attorney a few weeks to show cause for why Count 4 should not be dismissed—another opportunity for the judge to make me spend more money. By then, I knew Judge Merryday would spin more yarns and I would lose on Count 4, as well. Judge Merryday had managed my plaintiff's case similar to that of Mr. Del Fuoco.

On May 11, 2007, Judge Merryday finally got around to ruling on Count 4, granting "summary judgment" to the City, thereby affirming he identified no constitutional violations of law. He wrote the following, which was untruthful: *"The plaintiff also mischaracterized the factual record by repeatedly stating that the City's policy requires issuance of a ticket 'after every crash,' because of some indirect financial interest by the City and that this 'policy' explains Orban's citation."*

It is unclear how the judge could be confused about the existence of Tampa's ticket-at-every-crash policy or the large increase in tickets, since the "extra" police pension benefits legislation was passed in 1999. The judge misrepresented the insurance kickback arrangement as "some indirect financial interest to the City," never using the words "insurance" or "police pension" in his rulings. In reality, it is a direct financial kick-back to police administrators who establish the quotas. A *jury*, not an unscrupulous federal court judge, should have decided whether a $1 billion auto insurance increase in Tampa over 10 years was significant or insignificant.

Despite Officer Bowden explaining the expectation for a ticket at every crash in his deposition, Judge Merryday also wrote the following untrue statement: *"Moreover, Officer Bowden testified the City has no policy requiring the mandatory issuance of a citation."*

In his Count 4 (due process violations) ruling, Judge Merryday stated that I believed the ticket was issued in retaliation over the firing of Officer M.—something he failed to mention when ruling on Count 2 and 3 (malicious prosecution). Further, Judge Merryday wrote that I said the officer told me there was no traffic law violation, and therefore I am alleging malicious prosecution in Count 4, which he never disclosed in his rulings on Counts 2 and 3. It becomes evident why he separated his rulings. They contradict each other.

Judge Merryday again engaged in a discussion of the rear-end presumption law, all in the context of who pays for damages. He even mentions such cases proceeding "to a jury," which has nothing to do with traffic tickets, but rather jury trials over who pays damages. He was essentially concluding that who pays for damages is synonymous with violating a traffic law, just as Ralph Nader had pointed out, back in 1965, was the perspective of proprietary corporate interests. Since someone will pay for damages in all cases, Judge Merryday's belief supports a ticket at every crash.

The judge quoted from another case as follows: *"If the rear driver produces sufficient evidence to rebut the presumption, the case is submitted to the jury without the aid of the presumption, to reconcile and evaluate the credibility of the witnesses and the weight of the evidence."* If grading this as a college paper, I would tell Judge Merryday he is "off topic." His statement pertains to the process followed when the trailing driver (or their insurance company) is sued for not paying damages by alleging mitigating circumstances, a jury trial that has nothing to do with traffic tickets. Judge Merryday suggests the officers are ticketing to initiate some legal action relative to the rear-end presumption law, which is nonsense. Unfortunately, Judge Merryday did *not* seem to know the law. In reality, officers determine traffic violations only and insurance companies determine who will pay damages.

The judge further wrote the following statement, cited from another case: *"Police officers at the scene of an accident are neither permitted nor required to adjudicate the issue of fault (with an attendant risk of federal civil rights litigation in the event of a dispute) before issuing a traffic citation."* This contradicts the judge's belief that officers issue tickets to an *at fault* driver and makes it clear officers are not permitted to determine the issue of fault.

Judge Merryday concluded, *"Any suggestion that she is deprived of her constitutional rights is not only false, but moot."* By this point, I regarded Judge Merryday as moot, and do not understand why he is allowed to continue as a federal judge, after his transparent case-fixing on behalf of the Tampa Police Department and auto insurance industry.

With regard to the secret submission of crash reports to court, Judge Merryday endorsed the notion that a county traffic judge can send a memo to law enforcement agencies informing them they need not abide by Florida law, which is obviously untrue.[54] Judge Merryday did not perceive a problem with the *secret* submission of false

---

54 Judge Merryday wrote: *"Orban's further allegation of constitutional injury resulting from the City's 'policy' of allowing officers to submit 'crash reports' is equally moot and otherwise without merit. The Senior Administrative Judge for the Traffic Division for the City specifically allows officers of the police department to submit reports in place of live testimony. Orban twice challenged the allegation of the police report and achieved the dismissal of her citation, despite the existence of these allegedly 'false' report."*

police reports to court, and never mentioned Florida law prohibits the use of crash reports as evidence in court or that it is a crime to provide false information on crash reports. It was truly disturbing that a federal judge believed a county traffic judge (who was later disbarred after being charged with bank fraud) can write a *"memo"* informing law enforcement agencies that they need not abide by Florida law.

Judge Merryday also endorsed Tampa's ticket quota.[55] He referenced a case regarding a ticket quota in North Carolina, which was dissimilar to my case, as it was a law enforcement officer suing over expectations that he must meet the ticket quota. Further, Judge Merryday did not disclose that the North Carolina quotas lawsuit was dismissed and it stated the following about ticket quotas: *"To be sure, the alleged ticket quota policy makes a law enforcement officer's job more difficult. We are also sure that is not enough, standing alone, to constitute a substantive due process violation. A general order forbids officers from issuing citations for anything short of definite clear cut, substantial violations."*

In contrast to this case, I was not *theorizing* that the ticket quotas might result in traffic ticket fraud, but provided evidence that Tampa's ticket quotas resulted in ticket and crash reporting fraud, which Judge Merryday ignored.

Judge Merryday concluded that my complaint did not show an actual "injury" (meaning he did not regard my nearly $4,000 in additional insurance expense due to the false crash report as damages) and that I did not show a causal relation between the alleged injury and

---

55 Judge Merryday also wrote the following.

*"A plaintiff seeking to assert a substantive due process claim must allege the deprivation of a cognizable interest in life, liberty, or property; a mere allegation of 'arbitrary' government conduct in the air, so to speak, will not suffice* Gravitte v. North Carolina Division of Motor Vehicles, 2002. *A challenge to the* **City's ticket issuance policy** *simply fails... (finding that a North Carolina* **"ticket quota"** *policy violated neither the due process nor the privileges and immunities clauses of the Constitution). At most, Orban was inconvenienced by her citation appeals. Simply stated, a 'citizen does not suffer a constitutional injury every time [s]he is subject to the petty harassment of a state agent.'"*

the challenged act. He suggested my allegations were "hypothetical" and noted that one cannot seek an injunction for situations one has not experienced. He concluded, *"Orban fails to allege a constitutional injury and her inconvenience in defending the allegedly malicious prosecution is an insufficient basis for a section 1983 claim."*

Judge Merryday closed by writing I did not meet any of the four elements for a due process violation complaint, whereas I conclude all four were met.

Despite federal court having many rules, Judge Merryday was allowed to ignore facts and engage in misstatements and falsities to bolster his rulings. This may occur if a judge assumes no one will read the motions, affidavits, and depositions from the case, making it easy to hide the real issues. Anyone who reads Judge Merryday's rulings would assume I engaged in some negligent driving behavior and then filed a federal lawsuit over being ticketed. The judge failed to disclose statements made by the police chief, Officer Bowden, the retired sergeant's affidavit, and the affidavits of others who alleged ticket fraud. He simply regurgitated statements made by City of Tampa attorneys, which is why it is not possible to beat City Hall.

# CHAPTER 11

# THE APPELLATE COURT

## Reversing the Outcome
## While Pretending Not To

*"Dr. Orban is no more entitled to prospective relief than any other citizen of Tampa, and her undifferentiated, speculative claim cannot sustain federal jurisdiction. The district court thus properly DISMISSED Dr. Orban's due process claim for lack of standing."*

Appellate Judges Gerald Bard Tjoflat,
R. Lanier Anderson, and Susan H. Black
Their ruling on Count 4 of *Orban v. City of Tampa*
2008

After Judge Merryday's ruling on Count 4, Mr. Magri suggested I appeal his rulings, as he seemed confident of a win in a jury trial. At first, I was ambivalent, as prevailing on appeal meant returning to Judge Merryday's courtroom, where he would preside over a jury trial, deciding what evidence is allowed. If he deemed the officers' annual evaluations were "too prejudicial" to permit as evidence, the likelihood of winning would be reduced, and more money would have to be invested trying to get an appellate court to overturn such a ruling.

By then, I knew that Affiliated Computer Services (ACS) advertised that the federal court system used their *Agile*Jury product, which is the IT system that can be modified for local "business" needs on the presumption that some processes need "customizing." What jury pool would this software produce in the Middle District of Florida? Further, Judge Merryday would select a jury from the jury pool generated by the ACS system. My sense was a biased jury would be selected.

Nonetheless, a few factors motivated me to appeal Judge Merryday's verdicts on Counts 2, 3 and 4. I was confident that, if sent to a jury trial, the City would mediate (meaning change their policies), since they left the option open. Second, by filing my lawsuit, I had made things worse for Florida residents. Judge Merryday's rulings suggest that *any* rear-end crash, regardless of circumstances, is de facto careless driving—great news for auto insurers and "extra" police pension benefits. Further, Judge Merryday ruled ticket quotas were legal, despite the evidence they resulted in fraud. He also sanctioned the secret submission of crash reports to court, including false reports, despite this violating Florida law. Finally, intellectual curiosity persisted regarding what appellate judges would do with Judge Merryday's nonsense rulings that upheld Tampa's policies and practices as legal, including ticketing *at-fault* drivers. Judge Merryday's conclusions were not credible, since the Tampa police were not abiding by existing laws. *What would the appellate court do with Judge Merryday granting summary judgment on Count 4, as it seemed unlikely they would uphold it?*

My attorney filed a motion to the appellate court in November 2007 appealing Counts 2 and 3 (Malicious Prosecution) and Count 4 (Due Process Violations). On Count 4, I assumed the appellate court options were either to uphold Judge Merryday's ruling granting summary judgment (which sanctioned ticket quotas, secret crash report testimony, false crash reporting, and kickbacks from insurance companies to "extra" police pension benefits), or to send it back for a jury trial. I did not perceive any other options, and did not believe they would uphold Judge Merryday's ruling.

The City's attorneys responded with their same old arguments. They continued to be untruthful, again stating the judge initially found me "*Guilty* of *Careless Driving*." They know this is untrue, but apparently know if they write it, federal judges will repeat it. It was disconcerting that the federal appellate judges not only allowed the City's attorneys to make false statements, but they repeated some. The City attorneys wrote that I engaged in "*imaginative assertions of fantastical conspiracies and/or schemes to fund the Tampa Police Officers' Pension Fund.*" Then, they claimed I should be attacking Florida law that allows insurance premium revenues to fund "extra" police pension benefits. They also wrote "*Judge Merryday's holding took notice of Dr. Orban's specious argument that the Officers should not have found her not at fault.*" It was astounding they could not comprehend they are *not* determining fault, calling into question: are Tampa's City attorneys ignorant or corrupt?

The appellate court ordered a second mediation. It was vindictive, simply creating more expense for me in attorney fees. If the City of Tampa would not mediate prior to Judge Merryday's ruling, why would the three appellate judges believe they might do so after winning summary judgment on Counts 2, 3 and 4? The same materials were submitted to the second mediation, which was held at the federal courthouse. Similar to the first mediation, I asked for someone from the mayor's office to be present. Instead, the City sent Major John Bennett to the mediation.

Once Mr. Magri and I were alone with the mediator, she provided her personal criticisms of my appeal. Personal criticisms are not part of the mediation process and therefore can be repeated publicly. The mediator disparaged me for appealing Judge Merryday's rulings and said my appeal was hopeless. She turned to Mr. Magri and asked if he told me the appellate court overturns only 11 percent of rulings. Mr. Magri had told me it was less than 50 percent, which was technically correct. The woman did not understand the percentage did not matter to me. I was interested in assessing the integrity and credibility of the appellate court, and whether they would let Officer Bowden speak for himself, through his deposition, or continue to allow City attorneys to speak for him.

In March 2008, Mr. Magri called to say the appellate court affirmed Judge Merryday's rulings, which was hard to believe. However, as evidenced by the quotation that begins this chapter, federal appellate judges Gerald Bard Tjoflat, R. Lanier Anderson, and Susan H. Black were simply untruthful about Judge Merryday's ruling on Count 4. They pretended Judge Merryday had dismissed this count, whereas in reality Judge Merryday had granted summary judgment, which would have allowed the Tampa police to continue their unlawful practices.[56] A major lesson learned from my lawsuit is that federal district and appellate court judges are not held accountable for telling the truth.

In an opening line, the appellate judges wrote, "*Dr. Orban was at fault and guilty of careless driving because she failed to observe the stopped traffic in time to avoid a collision.*" They went beyond "probable cause" to say I was guilty of careless driving, even though my ticket was dismissed. This was strategic on their part by misrepresenting the verdict on my ticket. The word "guilty" has a specific meaning in court, so the appellate judges were attempting to mislead anyone who reads their ruling, most importantly to assure my case would never by overturned by the U.S. Supreme Court.

Similar to Judge Merryday, the appellate court judges simply parroted statements made by the City attorneys. They said probable cause existed due to the officers' "reasonably trustworthy information," identical to Judge Merryday's statement. They falsely stated, "*TPD's policy does not mandate that TPD officers issue a citation whenever they respond to an accident.*" Similar to Judge Merryday, the appellate judges ignored the deposition of Officer Bowden and the affidavit from the retired sergeant, which explained Tampa's ticket-at-every-crash policy. This occurred *despite* Mr. Magri pointing out that Officer Bowden's deposition was being ignored.

The three appellate judges concluded as follows: *To the extent Dr. Orban requests prospective relief against the City's alleged illegal scheme, she lacks standing; because even if she had established a violation of her constitutional right, she nevertheless failed to demonstrate a sufficient likelihood that she will be wronged again in a similar way.*

I never sought "prospective relief," so this is another falsity put forward by the trio of judges. Prospective relief was a fabrication created by City of Tampa attorneys and repeated by the federal judges. In reality,

---

56 The rulings from Judge Merryday and the appellate judges are available under the Cast of Characters link at: www.highwayrobberytampa.com.

my lawsuit attempted to resolve whether 11 Tampa police policies and practices were illegal and unconstitutional. I sought relief for all Tampa residents by attempting to have the court require the City of Tampa to change its policies to abide by Florida laws for all citizens. The officers who planned to testify in my case wanted this as well. In my opinion, because the appellate judges used falsities to rationalize their ruling, they were "guilty" of perjury and obstruction of justice.

Further, the appellate judges wrote, *"We express no opinion about whether Dr. Orban has established the violation of a federally protected right."* My lawsuit specified 11 Tampa police practices my attorney identified as unconstitutional and illegal based on laws and case law. In response, the appellate judges opted to render no opinion on whether these practices are illegal, and instead pretended Judge Merryday dismissed Count 4 due to lack of standing, whereas the judge had actually sanctioned the 11 practices by granting summary judgment to the City.[57]

---

57 Once again, my lawsuit identified the following 11 Tampa police practices as unconstitutional and illegal:

1. The City's policies, practices and customs to write a traffic citation without reasonable and probable grounds.
2. The issuance of citations, after it has been determined that issuance of a citation is inappropriate.
3. A practice of allowing a supervisor to override a determination of an officer investigating at the scene, in the absence of facts showing the supervisor had reasonable and probable grounds to cause a citation to issue.
4. Placing known erroneous entries in a citation or crash report to supply a rationale for the citation.
5. Traffic court use of crash reports to contradict the testimony of witnesses without providing said report to the parties and without appearance and authentication by the police officer.
6. A *de facto* quota system for traffic citations.
7. A system which causes citations to be issued to generate funds for the Police Pension Fund.
8. The practice of reducing employee or city contributions to the pension fund, based upon premium tax revenues received.
9. The practice of having insurance companies contribute to the police pension funds, based upon a percentage of premiums collected.
10. The practice and policy of keeping police officers away from court and not honoring subpoenas.
11. Refusing to give information to citizens that is required to be given, so the citizen can protest citations.

At the conclusion of their ruling, the appellate trio stated they "AF-FIRMED" Judge Merryday's ruling on Count 4 as having dismissed my lawsuit. However, they misrepresented Judge Merryday's ruling. For example, Judge Merryday had written, "*The City's motion for summary judgment on count four is GRANTED.*" By granting summary judgment, Judge Merryday ruled "*there are no issues of genuine material fact, there were not constitutional violations, and therefore there can be no cause of action against*" the City of Tampa. However, on Count 4, the appellate court wrote AFFIRMED and stated the following: *The district court thus properly DISMISSED Dr. Orban's due process claim for lack of standing.* The appellate judges simply lied about Judge Merryday's ruling. Dismissing my complaint means failing to have standing in court, which allowed the appellate judges to avoid making conclusions about Tampa's 11 practices that my lawsuit contended were illegal and unconstitutional. This was *creative dishonesty*, as they avoided a jury trial by being untruthful about Judge Merryday's ruling.

The appellate judges created a more favorable outcome for citizens, because they left unanswered the constitutionality of Tampa's ticket quotas, ticket-at-every-crash policy, false crash reporting, secret submission of crash reports to court, and the kick-back between auto insurance companies and "extra" police pension benefits.

Further, the appellate judges made their ruling an "unpublished opinion." Unpublished opinions cannot be used in future court cases, meaning another Florida city cannot use the rulings from my case in a related case. In essence, the appellate judges concluded, "*This stinks, don't bring it back*"... in recognition that Judge Merryday's rulings did *stink*, as he sanctioned Tampa's perverse police policies. An attorney could be held in contempt of court for citing an unpublished ruling, which reveals all one needs to know about the quality of Judge Merryday's rulings. The appellate judges deliberately left the questions of constitutionality unanswered, thereby protecting the credibility of Judge Merryday and Tampa Police Department administrators and attorneys, which was more important to them than protecting the public from Tampa's unlawful policies.

Before filing the lawsuit, I thought the federal court was a place of truthfulness and integrity. By the conclusion, I viewed it as an expensive kangaroo court where pathologic lying prevailed. Mr. Merkle knew exactly what he was talking about when he said, *"It's a results oriented process today, fairness be damned."*

Officer Bowden called me after reading the newspaper article about my lawsuit's "dismissal" and asked, *What happened?*

My response was what my attorney told me: *The judges denied our day in court!* By not honestly disclosing the contents of Officer Bowden's deposition, the judges failed to reveal Officer Bowden and I were on the same side. In fact, he had telephone discussions with my attorney and me following his deposition. In addition, many Tampa officers told me they looked forward to testifying about Tampa's quotas for the purpose of having them discontinued. However, it was more important to the three appellate judges to create the appearance the justice system in Tampa was "just," rather than to tell the truth.

Years earlier, an attorney explained the problem any court would have with my allegations and evidence. If it becomes common knowledge police officers are trained or permitted to engage in fraud and fabrications to advance traffic ticket convictions, as I alleged, then the integrity of the entire criminal justice system is called into question, since it relies on testimony from these same officers. However, the integrity of the criminal justice system is already being criticized, as Innocence Commissions are working to reverse death row convictions that occurred, in part, from fabrications and obfuscation by law enforcement officers, prosecutors and judges.[58]

Appellate Judges Gerald Bard Tjoflat, R. Lanier Anderson, and Susan H. Black, Judge Merryday and Magistrate Mark Pizzo marginalized all law enforcement officers by not allowing them to speak for

---

58 Jon Gould's book *The Innocence Commission* explained the problem that existed in Chicago as follows:
"Collectively the results were shocking. The *Tribune's* investigation alone found nearly 400 cases where prosecutors obtained homicide convictions by committing the most unforgiveable kinds of deception. They hid evidence that could have set defendants free. They allowed witnesses to lie. All in defiance of the law."

themselves. Instead, they allowed the City's attorneys to do the talking. The judges merely "parroted" what City of Tampa attorneys wrote. All five judges exhibited blatant disrespect for the law enforcement officers who had concerns about Tampa's perverse policies and practices.

Meanwhile, around the time the appellate court reviewed my case, the Tampa Police Department changed its policies—discontinuing writing tickets in minor accidents and abandoning the notion they were ticketing based on fault. This suggests the appellate court may have intervened to remedy corrupt Tampa police practices, but it is unknown how or why Tampa's policies were changed.

Accountability in federal court needs to be improved, especially since federal judges can create case law that deviates from existing laws, as Judge Merryday attempted to do. Federal judges must be held accountable for telling the truth and for avoiding overt bias. While systems are designed to assure federal judges avoid political influence, a total lack of accountability fosters untruthfulness and omissions of relevant evidence, as I experienced.

At present, federal judges get a free pass on the source of their information. Judge Merryday and the appellate judges made numerous claims about what Officer Bowden and I said, but they were not taken from the original source. As my lawsuit illustrates, attorneys for the City of Tampa engaged in fabrications and misrepresentations. Then, the federal judges repeated some falsities and misrepresentations by quoting from the City's attorneys, pretending their statements were true.

To advance accountability, *federal judges should be required to use in-text references to demonstrate where their evidence was derived.* And *it should be mandatory that only the primary source can be used.*

For example, Judge Merryday and the appellate judges wrote I was found guilty on the traffic ticket, because attorneys for the City of Tampa wrote this in their court filings. If required to provide an in-text citation that references the original source, the judges would have been forced to use the court document that provided the actual outcome, instead of the City attorneys' fabrication.

In addition, *any evidence that was submitted, but not used in a judge's ruling, should be listed in an "Omitted Evidence List."* Such a list in my lawsuit would reveal Judge Merryday and the appellate judges essentially took all of their information from City of Tampa attorneys, while omitting essentially all evidence submitted by my attorney, thereby revealing an extraordinary bias. In my case, the omitted evidence included my attorney's legal theories, the depositions of Officer Bowden and Police Chief Hogue, my affidavit and deposition, the affidavit from the retired sergeant, affidavits from citizens who reported being victims of Tampa police crash reporting fraud, and my traffic expert's reconstruction of my accident circumstances.

A federal complaint system is needed to allow plaintiffs and defendants to make complaints about a federal judge, but not the usual *circling the wagons* "internal affairs" process. The proposed references and omissions lists are essential to an effective complaint system. Federal lawsuits produce boxes of paper that would be time-consuming to review if a complaint is made. Knowing the source of a judge's statement (or what was omitted) would make a complaint process much more straightforward.

At a minimum, *the U.S. Department of Justice, at the national level, should investigate complaints that a federal judge or appellate judge was untruthful.* A credible complaint system may deter federal judges from engaging in the behaviors exhibited in my case, especially if their beloved federal pensions were put at risk for untruthfulness.

## CHAPTER 12

# THE SURPRISING NEXUS OF POLICING FOR PROFIT IN TAMPA

*"Unless the officer sees the accident, a citation will not be written, unless there is a severe injury, DUI or one of the drivers leaves the scene."*

Laura McElroy
Tampa police spokesperson
Reported on November, 11, 2008 by WTSP news

The Tampa Police Department abandoned their ticket-at-every-crash policy around the time the appellate court reviewed my lawsuit. Officer Bowden told me officers had been retrained. He said if my minor accident occurred in the present time, he would be prohibited from writing a ticket or the long-form crash report that was used by my auto insurance company to charge nearly $4,000 in additional premiums. Also, since the conclusion of my lawsuit in 2008, I have never observed Tampa's traffic squad officers working in wolf packs. Speed traps simply vanished from the streets of Tampa. Nonetheless, these two policy changes did nothing to deter the Tampa Police Department from policing for profit.

While the number of non-criminal moving violation tickets decreased following my lawsuit, the Tampa police still had 121,000 traffic citations in 2013 and another 60,000 red-light camera tickets—more tickets than ever before. More importantly, criminal traffic violations increased, which result in an arrest. The Tampa police were arresting as many people as ever. In 2013, they had 22,000 arrests for violent and non-violent crimes and another 25,000 for criminal traffic violations. Most traffic arrests (20,000) were for driving with a suspended or expired license, which was 10,000 more such arrests than in 2005. The State no longer reported "miscellaneous" arrests, meaning Tampa's total number of arrests is unknown. In 2013, the Tampa police had at least 47,000 arrests (crime plus traffic), which continues at one arrest for every 7.4 Tampa residents annually. Further, the Tampa police were producing more court cases than ever, more than 200,000 annually—one court case for every 1.7 Tampa residents.

It was possible to determine the nexus of the City of Tampa's perverse practices to advance convictions and auto insurance interests. As explained in the book, *Cigar City Mafia: A Complete History of the Tampa Underworld*, organized crime requires only one person in a key position in a police department to meet "crooked" needs, such as relaying confidential information about investigations. Similarly, proprietary interests, such as auto insurance interests, would need only one person in a key position to advance policing for profit policies and practices. It relies on a hub and spoke model. The hub (nexus) creates policies and expectations, and the spokes implement them, not necessarily understanding the implications. *The hub—who can it be?*

John Bennett appears an obvious choice, but it was not him. In 2000, he was merely an aide to the police chief when he blocked efforts to resolve my complaint about ticket and crash reporting fraud. He was being trained in policing for profit, but was not the ringleader. Bennett was moved into administration and parroted whatever nonsense he was told, e.g., increasing traffic tickets reduces crashes and red-light cameras save lives. Likely unknown to Bennett, he was set-up as the "fall guy" should my complaint about police practices ever be investigated by State or federal authorities, deflecting from the real nexus.

Tampa's police chiefs are potential choices. Initially, I thought it was Police Chief Holder, since he initiated the practice of evaluating officers based on annual numbers of tickets issued when policing for profit began in 1999. Also, he promoted officers with behavior or performance issues—which seemed parallel to joining a gang where one must steal a car to become a member—thereby enhancing control over the wrongdoers.

However, in 2003, under Mayor Pam Iorio, the entire Tampa police top administration completely turned over. Prior to the election, her campaign manager told me she planned to do this, since a judge told her it was needed. Under Mayor Iorio, the old police administration was gone, yet nothing improved. Despite the retirement of Police Chief Holder and two assistant chiefs, as well as eliminating the three deputy chief positions, policing for profit in Tampa grew more aggressive, suggesting the nexus was not Chief Holder.

The deposition of Chief Holder's successor, Police Chief Hogue, reveals he was not the "culprit." He presented as a polite, but vapid man in his deposition, albeit quite keen on tickets and arrests. Nonetheless, he said false crash reports should be corrected and crash reports should be written based on what an officer is told, if the circumstances fit. He candidly disclosed that, until I came along, he actually believed the police were paid by insurance companies to investigate crashes, which was the rationale for requiring a ticket at every crash. He had been misinformed about the law regarding police investigations of crashes. Further, he admitted to being clueless about citizen complaints regarding his police department.

What about Tampa's mayors? Mayors Dick Greco and Pam Iorio are very different. Greco was the mayor when policing for profit began in 1999. However, he had retained existing department heads upon becoming mayor in 1995, including Police Chief Holder, allowing the police department to manage its affairs. Officers report they had good access to Mayor Greco, such that he is not linked to advancing any particular police agenda. Further, officers told me he did not endorse the large (40%) pension benefit increase proposed by the police union, perceiving it as unaffordable. He was a businessman and would understand the extraordinary long term costs.

Some police officers believed Mayor Iorio, elected in 2003, expected Police Chief Hogue to lower crime rates to bolster her apparent effectiveness, which resulted in the Tampa police underreporting certain crimes. Mayor Iorio may not have known about this, if simply focusing on the end, rather than the means. She obviously knew of my issues, since my lawsuit was reported in newspapers, and yet she allowed the quotas to continue. However, policing for profit pre-dates her and she simply allowed it to continue, meaning she is not the nexus. Further, Mayor Iorio had a dilemma, in that she was touting lower crime rates as her big mayoral success story, a claim that could quickly vanish if subsequently criticizing police practices over ticket and arrest quotas that resulted in fraud and fabrications.

Who does this leave as the nexus, the hub?

It was obvious all along, but became transparent in a 2009 news article. A U.S. Supreme Court case revealed Tampa police officers were instructed to read Miranda rights, which inform arrested persons of their constitutional rights, in a way that obfuscates the person's right to an attorney while being questioned by the police. Ultimately, the U.S. Supreme Court decided, in a split 7-2 decision, that the Tampa police procedure was acceptable. However, the source of the Tampa police obfuscation practice was revealed in a *Tampa Tribune* news article. The person advocating for obfuscation in reading Miranda rights was Kirby Rainsberger—Tampa's police attorney.[59]

---

59 The *Tampa Tribune* reported the following:

"*Local defense lawyers are angry over a Tampa Police Department memorandum outlining the department's approach when reading people Miranda rights. The memo, written by Tampa police legal adviser Kirby Rainsberger states that in certain situations where a suspect needs to be questioned, only the first line, "You have the right to remain silent and anything you say can be used against you in court," is good enough. The second line, which informs a person of his or her right to an attorney, can wait until the suspect is willing to talk, the memo states. Although police say this is nothing new, Tampa-based defense lawyer said the memo urges officers to be tricky by splitting up the Miranda warnings. "They are trying to usurp people's constitutional rights," He said, "It's not a game and it's not a technicality. These are*

The purpose of the obfuscation was to advance convictions among suspects. Tampa's police spokesperson explained, "*Officers don't have to read a suspect his or her Miranda rights if they have probable cause to make an arrest,*" supposedly for the purpose of keeping criminals off the streets.

From my perspective, the nexus of improper Tampa police practices is Mr. Rainsberger, with help from other City of Tampa attorneys who assisted in advancing policing for profit. Ideally, a police attorney should inform the police chief and mayor of policies and procedures that adhere to laws, rather than encouraging policies and practices that ignore laws, sometimes under the guise of "home rule," to advance tickets, arrests and convictions.

As further evidence, Bennett's 2001 e-mail to Mayor Greco reported that their legal counsel concurred that my false reporting complaint need not be investigated, recognizing Mr. Rainsberger was their legal counsel. Their failure to investigate my complaint violated Tampa's written policy, Florida law, and CALEA accreditation standards. Further, Rainsberger wrote the letter to my attorney stating he

---

*rights under the Constitution every person has." The method outlined in the June 30 memo gives officers several opportunities to get information from a person in custody. If officers "routinely blurt out Miranda warnings for no particular reason and the suspect equally thoughtlessly says he'll take the free lawyer, the latent investigators have just lost their best opportunity to help resolve the case, and perhaps many others," Rainsberger writes. Once a person requests an attorney, law enforcement can no longer question them unless his or her attorney is present. Before questioning a suspect, once the first Miranda line is read, "stop right there," Rainsberger says. "Ask the suspect if he wants to talk about the matter now. If he says 'No,' go no further with the rights advisement of the interview." An amended version of the memo was sent out on July 28 and includes suggestions on when officers can approach a suspect without his attorney present and try questioning him again. Assistant Public Defender John Skye said Tampa police's Miranda procedures have two problems. "First of all, that's not what you're supposed to be doing," Skye said. "You're supposed to be telling people of their constitutional rights, not trying to trick them. The other thing is if you succeed and the whole truth comes out, then it seems much more likely to me that the statement would be suppressed." Tampa police disagree and say how they recite Miranda rights is nothing new. "This is a tool to keep criminals off the street," police spokeswoman Andrea Davis said. Officers don't have to read a suspect his or her Miranda rights if they have probable cause to make an arrest, she said."*

concurred my crash report had errors, but refused to amend them, which is contrary to Florida law. It was the false crash report that created thousands of dollars in additional insurance expense to me, and it was Rainsberger who personally refused to correct the errors, at a time my insurance company offered to refund the money if the report was corrected. Rainsberger wrote that my crash report did not need to be corrected, since the hearing was over; suggesting he was unconcerned that a judge used a false crash report in a court proceeding.

From my perspective, the use of false crash reports to advance convictions is similarly dishonest as the intentional delay in informing arrested persons of their right to an attorney for the purpose of advancing convictions. Both are policing for profit tactics. Rainsberger's letter to my attorney stated that crash reports are inadmissible in court, and yet he knew that Tampa Police Department's written policy allowed their submission to court as secret evidence. Also, he would know that the police department was not paid by insurance companies to investigate crashes, while nonetheless allowing officers and the police chief to believe they were.

Rainsberger was not alone. In their motion for summary judgment, Tampa's City Attorney David L. Smith and Assistant City Attorney Ursula Richardson wrote that *why* an accident occurred is not a factor in the ticketing decision, a statement that is clearly contrary to Florida law. Further, Ms. Richardson also refused to amend the false report.

It was attorneys for the Tampa police who made false statements in the City's motions in federal court, which Judge Merryday and the appellate judges merely regurgitated. Attorneys for the Tampa Police Department persuaded Judge Merryday to rule in favor of ticketing *at fault* drivers, rather than drivers who violate a traffic law. The City's attorneys would know that *fault* is inadmissible as evidence in traffic ticket hearings. Further, Ms. Richardson knew all the details of my court case, knew what I requested in mediation because she attended, and yet she *never* attempted to mediate or resolve a single issue—all to the advantage of the auto insurance industry.

Thus, it was Kirby Rainsberger and other attorneys for the Tampa Police Department who were the nexus of policing for profit, and not police administrators. Their efforts ultimately created more jobs for attorneys, while also advancing proprietary interests. Rainsberger, Richardson, Smith, and the City's external counsel advanced proprietary interests while creating a "jobs program" for local attorneys, prosecutors and judges.

Clearly, the City of Tampa has no capacity for improvement until securing legal counsel that advances and informs officials on lawful and best practices. The quality and integrity of one's legal counsel is a barometer for the quality and integrity of a law enforcement agency's policies and practices.

# CHAPTER 13

# REASONS WHY THE U.S. IS THE INCARCERATION NATION

*"I will ask again, Who will stop corruption here in Tampa? Who has the guts?"*

Ad appearing in the *St. Petersburg Times*
(a.k.a. *Tampa Bay Times*)
November 2009

In 2015 (seven years after my lawsuit concluded), news sources began to raise concerns about Tampa's policing for profit tactics—*better late than never*. In 2015, a news story reported the Tampa Police Department's arrest rate per 1000 population was double to triple that of other major cities in central Florida. Black residents accounted for more than half the arrests, despite comprising only 26% of the population.

Also, in 2015, a *Tampa Bay Times* analysis reported that, since 2008, the Tampa police have been targeting bicyclists in low income neighborhoods for traffic violations—2,500 bike tickets in recent years. The bicycle tickets were for minor infractions, such as not having a bike light or transporting a second person on the handlebars with 80% issued to black residents. In one case, a Tampa officer took possession of a bike because the black bicyclist did not have proof of purchase, even though the bicycle was not reported as stolen. Sometimes, officers used the bicycle stops to ask about drug possession, thereby producing arrests.

Tampa's police chief, Jane Castor, postured that ticketing and arresting low income residents in high crime neighborhoods is how the Tampa police reduced violent and non-violent crime rates. However, in 2015, an epidemic of murders occurred in these same neighborhoods. Following public outcry, Tampa's police chief and Mayor Bob Buckhorn requested an investigation from the U.S. Department of Justice over the bicycle tickets. Meanwhile, Mayor Buckhorn declined to comment on the news story about Tampa's high arrest rate.

The malicious reality is that the Tampa Police Department, and other law enforcement agencies who use similar policing for profit tactics, are creating a permanent underclass among lower income citizens. The strategy begins with police officers issuing excessive numbers of traffic tickets, and more recently automated camera tickets. Red-light cameras and speed cameras can accelerate the development of a permanent underclass, especially when cameras are placed in low-income neighborhoods and coupled with roadway engineering defects (too low a speed limit or yellow light timings that are too short). Low-income drivers (or bicyclists) are less likely to afford the ticket fine.

When motorists cannot pay a ticket, their driver's license is often suspended. If continuing to drive with a suspended license, such as to work, they will be arrested and their vehicle impounded. If they cannot afford the initial ticket, it is unlikely they can afford the high impound fees, and hence their vehicle becomes the property of the police and the driver no longer has a vehicle, which can affect continued employment. This illustrates how an initial traffic ticket written to a lower income person can trigger a sequence whereby the driver ultimately ends up with an arrest record, which can affect future employment opportunities, more fines to pay, and no vehicle to get to their job.

This punitive "set up"—from the driver's or bicyclist's perspective—is entirely unnecessary, since a written warning that does not carry a fine can be used by police departments for minor offenses, and courts can require community service instead of cash payments when convicting low-income residents. However, these are not options if policing for profit.

Police departments that embrace policing for profit demonstrate human behavior reminiscent of the 1971 Stanford prison experiment, which found some individuals in positions of power enjoy taunting and punishing the powerless. Unfortunately, in Tampa, such officers are rewarded, because tickets and arrests—called "self-initiated" activity—result in promotions. By design, policing for profit is ultimately used to justify a larger and larger justice system (more officers, judges and attorneys), and more opportunities to generate money and punish the city's residents, in particular low income persons.

If the consequences from a ticket, or an arrest for a minor violation, eventually result in unemployment due to lack of transportation or an arrest record, the likelihood increases that crime, including drug dealing, may be used to support oneself, which then necessitates more arrests for these crimes. It is a self-perpetuating cycle among police, where arrests and tickets issued to lower income persons result in unpaid fines or driving with a suspended license, which can lead to more arrests. CompStat-like systems that endorse arresting individuals for minor offenses create communities with more and more people possessing lengthy arrest records. Inevitably, such a skewed "approach to justice" is a war against the poor.[60]

Further, drug possession offenses can result in lengthy prison sentences that are disproportionate to the severity of the crime. In an *NPR* report, a sheriff explained the rationale for such disproportionately long sentences. If law enforcement believes someone committed a serious crime, but they did not have the evidence to get a conviction, they can use a drug possession offense as an alternative

---

60 This is exacerbated when low income persons, who cannot afford their bail, feel pressure to take a plea deal that requires them to plead guilty to a lesser charge in order to avoid remaining in jail until their trial occurs. Such "deals" can ultimately result in long criminal records even for those who were not guilty, but sensed coercion to accept a "deal."

to secure a lengthy prison sentence, which further reveals unfairness in the justice system. Even more, drug possession can create the risk of life in prison for minor offenses when *three-strikes-and-you're-out* laws are used.

The American Civil Liberties Union (ACLU) reports law enforcement agencies disproportionately target African American citizens, as they are incarcerated for drug possession at 10 times the rate of white persons. The ACLU supports abolishing or reforming mandatory minimum sentences for drug possession offenses, since they are unnecessarily harsh. Sustaining such sentences, which are disproportionate to the crime, creates expense for the public, due to the expanded number of inmates, while creating revenues and profits for the corporate interests that are prison system vendors—*the proprietary public safety establishment.*

In addition, a serious problem exists at all levels of government, among both elected and appointed officials, as some pursue a "*more for me*" philosophy, and a subset ultimately cross the line, becoming criminals as a consequence—thereby creating even more prison inmates that taxpayers must fund. In just one month's time around November 2009, newspapers reported on the cases of one corrupted public official after another—Judge Stringer's bank fraud, former NYPD Police Commissioner Bernard Kerik felonious acts, and a governor and a Congressman—all committing crimes.

An aide to Rod Blagojevich, the former governor of Illinois, pled guilty to wire fraud, admitting to discussions with the governor about using campaign contributions to create a fund that would be split among "the inner circle." In 2009, Blagojevich was the fourth of the most recent eight Illinois governors to be sentenced to prison. The others were found guilty of racketeering, bank fraud, and bribery, respectively. More recently, in 2014, a former governor of Virginia was sentenced to prison for two years on federal corruption charges that occurred while governor, although he is appealing.

In 2009, a former U.S. Congressman, William Jefferson, was sentenced to 13 years in prison for "repeated attempts to sell his office"—bribes, money laundering, and racketeering. His schemes were supposedly structured to net millions of dollars for himself. Of course, he is not the first in Congress to be found guilty of taking bribes. In 2007, a former House Representative from Ohio was sentenced to more than two years for taking bribes from a lobbyist. In 2006, a California Congressman was sentenced for taking $2.4 million in bribes. In 2002, yet another was sentenced to 7 years over bribes and racketeering. In 2009, *The Irish Times* described the problem as follows: *U.S. Congressmen tread a fine line between legitimate political fundraising and influence-peddling, between friendship with lobbyists and outright corruption.* In 2011, Jack Abramoff, the former lobbyist who served more than three years in federal prison, alleged that "very few" in Congress do not accept some form of bribery.

Corruption has even existed in the Florida prison system. In 2007, Florida's Secretary of the Department of Corrections and one of his regional directors were convicted for accepting $130,000 in kickbacks from a vendor who sold snacks and drinks to prisoners. The former Secretary was sentenced to 8 years in federal prison—transitioning from prison CEO to inmate.

In Florida, the problem was so pervasive that in 2009, the Florida Supreme Court granted Governor Charlie Crist's request to impanel a grand jury to investigate public corruption. This occurred after federal agents arrested three public officials in south Florida for taking bribes to advance certain business interests. At the time, Governor Crist had removed 30 corrupt officials in just three years—evidence something had seriously gone awry among public officials.

Unfortunately, the "call to public service" has morphed into a "more for me" philosophy among too many public officials.

As an example of the *more for me* philosophy among public officials in Tampa, albeit not a crime, Mayor Iorio used her autonomy as mayor to create large salary and pension benefit increases for herself, police officers, firefighters, and other employees, while preying on the public for more revenue from tickets and arrests, as well as increasing many other fees. Such generosity to themselves increases the need for policing for profit, as they must generate the revenue to fund the larger salaries and benefits.

In 2004, Mayor Iorio achieved legislative approval to increase Tampa Fire and Police pension benefits by 40%. She also gave the police large annual salary increases over a few years, which was about 40% once compounded. The 40% salary increase on top of a 40% pension benefit increase yielded an astounding 96% pension benefit increase for retiring police officers. The State estimated that both City and employee contributions to the pension would need to double or triple to fund the larger benefit, as it was not prorated, which increased the City's contribution rate from about 8% to 20% of each officer and firefighter's salary.[61] This necessitated nearly $10 million more in additional revenue annually to fund the pension increase for police officers and firefighters.

Mayor Iorio also increased the multiplier for the general City pension, which covers all other employees, giving them larger pensions, and changed the vesting period from 10 to six years. A 2-term Tampa mayor, such as herself, can now vest in the City pension plan, along with high-priced staff who come and go with each mayor. Then, she attempted to outsource some work provided by lower wage employees to avoid the cost of their health insurance and pension benefits, understanding that private businesses often do not provide health insurance or retirement benefits to lower wage workers, thus reducing their total compensation. This parallels a common private sector business model that handsomely rewards those at the top while being indifferent about the health and financial security of those toward the bottom of the pay scale.

As she neared the end of her second term, Mayor Iorio complained about the high cost of pension benefits, after a correct contribution rate was restored to the Tampa Fire and Police pension

---

61 However, for the majority of Mayor Iorio's eight years in office, the pension was underfunded, as the City's contribution rates declined to 1% and then subsequently increased to 2%, 3% and then 5%, revealing how a single autonomous public official can underfund a pension.

during her final year as mayor, but she never acknowledged her role in increasing the pension benefits. Mayor Iorio's salary and pension benefit increases reflect a dilemma in addressing America's crumbling infrastructure. Elected officials can choose to spend taxpayer money on needed infrastructure, or alternatively on themselves—salary and benefit increases, along with bonuses. Such increases create the need for additional revenue, which can be used to justify policing for profit.

In 2009, Tampa's police Chief Hogue abruptly retired without any fanfare. Mayor Iorio then appointed Tampa's first woman police chief. Would things be different? No, the police chief was Jane Castor, who attended my first mediation. Major John Bennett was promoted to Assistant Police Chief, in charge of overseeing police operations. They added 69,000 annual red-light camera tickets after Bob Buckhorn became mayor in 2011, and used the camera ticket revenue to help balance the City's budget.

In 2014, dishonest Tampa police officers became front page news. In less than a year, seven were fired, including a detective who stole money orders and checks from the evidence room ($101,000), a homicide detective accused of a tax fraud scheme, a sergeant who used the food stamps of a police informant, and an officer who had sex with an underage girl at the school he patrolled. A *more for me* attitude was evident among these Tampa police officers. Even Tampa's police chief accepted a *more for me* privilege near the time of her retirement, which deviated from Florida law, albeit sanctioned by City officials.

Chief Jane Castor was scheduled to retire in 2014, due to a retirement program she had entered, called DROP. If not retiring on time, per Florida law, she would lose $589,000 in deferred retirement (DROP) benefits that she would otherwise collect. Regardless, she kept her $156,000 police chief job for another year, while also reported to receive $113,000 in annual pension benefits, the $589,000 in DROP benefits, and $140,000 in unpaid vacation and sick leave due to her hypothetical retirement. This totaled about $1 million in compensation during her final year with the Tampa Police

Department.[62] Not surprisingly, her ability to retain the $589,000 in DROP retirement benefits was due to deviating from Florida law via "home rule." Mayor Buckhorn and the City Council postured that the police chief was retired, but also now employed as a "civilian," apparently making Florida law inapplicable.

In 2015, both Police Chief Castor and Assistant Police Chief John Bennett retired. Similar to Chief Castor, Bennett's time was up due to the DROP program, but he was not allowed to stay on as a "civilian," despite an attempt to do so.[63] The upshot of Castor staying on for an additional year was that John Bennett never became Tampa's police chief. Both will be remembered by some for their commitment to policing for profit, while amassing small fortunes for themselves under the pretense of "public service." Based on average life expectancy, both should reap their generous annual police pensions for as many years as they worked for the Tampa Police Department (approximately 30 years). Meanwhile, both retired amid news reports of the extraordinary number of Tampa Police Department arrests and bicycle tickets that disproportionately targeted low-income and black residents.

---

62 Chief Castor's $1 million compensation in her final year reflects Mayor Iorio's generous salary and pension increases. Without the large increase, Chief Castor's DROP benefit would have been around $300,000 and her annual pension about $60,000. Mayor Iorio's near doubling of pension benefits for officers was achieved absent a transparent plan to fund it. The not-so-transparent funding plan was the Florida legislature's change in the law in 1999 that rewards police with "extra" pension benefits if they increase auto insurance rates paid in their municipality. However, in Tampa, this funding was grossly inadequate to pay for the near doubling of pension benefits. The change in Florida law generated an additional $8 million for the police pension over the first 10 years, whereas the City needed to increase its contribution by nearly $10 million annually to cover the larger pension benefit for police officers and firefighters. Meanwhile, auto insurance companies netted about $1 billion more from Tampa drivers over these 10 years, giving them, by far, the largest bounty from policing for profit.

63 Subsequently, Mark Woodard, the husband of former Mayor Pam Iorio and the administrator for Pinellas County (Florida), hired John Bennett as an Assistant County Administrator at a $159,640 salary to preside over public health, safety and welfare. Time will tell whether Bennett advances policing for profit schemes in Pinellas County.

Thus, it is not surprising that in November 2009, a man paid for a half-page ad in the *St. Petersburg Times* titled, "Corruption in Tampa." His ad asks, *I will ask again, Who will stop corruption here in Tampa? Who has the guts?* He alleged many sources of corruption, including the police department, judges, and elected officials. From my experience, Tampa is sewn up quite tightly. There is nowhere to go to for help—not the police, the mayor, City Council members, City attorneys, the State Attorney, the Florida Department of Law Enforcement, the Florida Attorney General, the U.S. Attorney, or the federal court. However, all such public officials are not corrupt—some just *circle the wagons*.

Tampa's ticket and arrest quotas, and the related fraud, is particularly detrimental to lower income persons and demonstrate the need for improved accountability systems, because the "honor system" is not working in the so-called justice system. When police departments only promote officers who produce large numbers of tickets and arrests, policing for profit will ultimately be embraced by all in police administration, since they are the only people promoted. They were never encouraged, along the way, to use more effective and ethical approaches, such as community policing. Instead, they were promoted due to a willingness to perceive the general public as criminals and revenue sources—*to collect and serve, rather than to protect and serve.*

Questions remain for Tampa and the multitude of other policing for profit communities across the United States: *Who will stop them? Who has the guts?*

# APPENDIX A

| | NOTICE OF DISCIPLINARY ACTION | | Date Prepared 4/15/02 |
|---|---|---|---|

| Employee Name BUNCAN, David K. | Employee No. 44916 | Social Security No. On File | Position Title Police Officer | Pay Grade P-1 |
|---|---|---|---|---|

| Dept./Div. Name Police / District II | Dept. Hearing Date (If applicable) |
|---|---|

**EMPLOYEE STATUS**
- ☒ Regular
- ☐ Probationary
- ☐ Entrance
- ☐ Promotional
- ☐ Seasonal
- ☐ Temporary
- ☐ Other (Specify)

**BARGAINING UNIT STATUS**
- ☐ A.T.U. ☒ P.B.A.
- ☐ I.A.F.F. ☐ None

**REASONS FOR DISCIPLINARY ACTION**
- ☐ Incompetence
- ☒ Insubordination
- ☐ Neglect of Duty
- ☐ Moral Turpitude
- ☐ Breach of Peace
- ☐ Other (Specify)

State specific reasons and circumstances of the incident(s) which led to this action. Include names of any witnesses, time, location of incident and what happened and specific improvements expected, and what further action may be taken if improvements don't occur. This action should include accompanying documentation of previous written warnings, admonishments and suspensions.

DISCIPLINARY HISTORY

4/01/01    REPRIMAND    MR# 1402, 1102, & 1005  DEPT. PROPERTY RESTRICTION, STANDARD OF CONDUCT

On December 23, 2000 at approximately 1622 hours, Officer David Duncan was on duty in his marked unit riding with a reserve officer when they observed a white GMC Yukon matching the description of a stolen vehicle. Officer Duncan pulled behind the vehicle to verify that it was stolen. As he awaited confirmation from Communications, the passenger of the suspect vehicle exited the vehicle and ran away. Officer Duncan's reserve officer immediately exited the marked unit and gave chase. With the driver remaining in the suspect vehicle, Officer Duncan exited the marked unit, drew his service weapon and approached the driver in an attempt to gain compliance.

Officer Duncan's actions were in violation of SOP 831: Vehicle Stops - Felony/High Risk as he gave up his cover position and approached the driver on foot. SOP 831 requires that "both officers (two officer unit) remain at the cover position of their patrol car until all occupants are removed."

This disciplinary action is based on the nature of the violation and Officer Duncan's previous disciplinary history. Future violations similar in nature will be dealt with in a more stringent and progressive manner.

*(ATTACH ADDITIONAL SHEETS)*

**Disciplinary Action to be Taken:**
- ☒ Reprimand
- ☐ Suspension - Number of Work Days _____
  - Effective Date _____
  - Date Scheduled to return to work _____
- ☐ Dismissal - Effective Date _____
- ☐ Quit Without Notice (AWOL)
  - Effective Date: _____
- ☐ Disciplinary Demotion - Effective Date _____
  - New Position Title _____
  - New Pay Range _____
- ☐ Other _____

| Supervisor's Name | Date 5/11/02 | Department Director or Designee's Signature | Date 5/8/02 |
|---|---|---|---|

**Note to Employee:**
1. This is to inform you that disciplinary action is being taken for the above reasons.
2. Your acknowledgement of receipt does not indicate agreement.
3. See the reverse side for important information about your rights.

| Employee Signature | Date 5-11-02 |
|---|---|

**COMPLAINT REVIEW BOARD**
**LETTER OF NOTICE**

TO: _____DUNCAN, David K._____ DATE: _____April 15, 2002_____

Please be advised that in reference to an impending disciplinary action against you for an incident which constitutes a violation of Tampa Police Department Manual of Regulations, specifically:

SOP 831 - Vehicle Stops - Felony/High Risk

said violation is a matter which might result in your suspension, demotion or dismissal. Details of the allegation are as follows:

SEE ATTACHED DA-88.

Therefore, this notice is to advise you of your right to a Complaint Review Board. Should you desire a Complaint Review Board, a letter requesting same must be submitted to the undersigned Division Commander within three days. If the third day falls on a weekend or holiday, the letter may be submitted the following Monday or the first workday following the holiday.

If a Complaint Review Board is requested, your letter requesting it must list your two selections to serve on the board. Please determine their willingness to serve prior to submitting their names. You might also wish to review departmental SOP 641.2.

Any appeals to Civil Service or through collective bargaining grievance procedure may be made only after Notice of Disciplinary Action (DA 88) is served upon you advising of the final decision of the Chief of Police.

_____ 4/15/02          _____ 4-15-02
Division Commander                          Employee                    Date

Served by: _____     Date: _____4/15/02_____

TPD 612 (5/94)          White - Disciplinary File Copy; Yellow - Employee Copy          Printed on Recycled Paper

# Tampa Police Department
## Discipline History

*Emp Nbr*   44916   *Employee Name*   DUNCAN, DAVID K

| Date | Penalty | Violations | Comments |
|------|---------|-----------|----------|
| 4/1/01 | REPRIMAND | MR# 1402, #1102, #1005 | DEPT PROPERTY RESTRICTION, STANDARD OF CONDUCT |

169

COPY

February 25, 2002

TO: .        B. R. HOLDER
              Chief of Police

ATTN:      W. A. SAWYER
              Assistant Chief of Police

FROM:     KIRBY C. RAINSBERGER
              Assistant City Attorney

RE:         I.A.B. Case 00F-527
              Officer David K. Duncan

Sir:

     This is the disposition memorandum concluding the Internal Affairs investigation into the shooting death of Antonio Scott by Officer David K. Duncan which occurred on December 23, 2000. On that date at approximately 1622 hours, Officer Duncan was on duty in a marked unit together with Reserve Officer Brian Brundage when Brundage spotted a white GMC Yukon matching the description of a stolen vehicle on the most current hot sheet. The officers turned and attempted to catch up to the Yukon which was northbound on 40th Street from the intersection with Hillsborough Avenue. Officer Duncan was driving and used the overhead emergency lights of his patrol car intermittently to clear traffic in order to catch up to the Yukon. Upon getting close enough to read the Yukon's license plate, the officers confirmed that the plate matched the plate of the stolen Yukon on the hot sheet and requested by radio that Communications run a high speed check to verify that the vehicle had not been previously recovered. Before Communications could respond, the Yukon drove into the parking lot of a small shopping center located at 6425 N. 40th Street and stopped. This action was initiated by the Yukon driver inasmuch as the police vehicle was not displaying emergency lights at that time.

     The Yukon was facing east and was in a parking space immediately in front of the shopping center. Officer Duncan pulled in behind and roughly perpendicular to the Yukon. The police vehicle was stopped well behind the Yukon, too far behind to effectively block it in.

     The only passenger in the Yukon immediately opened the right front door and ran south with Officer Brundage close behind. Officer Duncan ran to the driver's side of the Yukon and drew his service weapon with his right hand. The driver's door remained closed as Duncan approached, pointed the firearm at the driver seated inside, and repeatedly ordered the driver to get out of the car. Upon getting no response, Duncan grabbed the driver's door handle with his left hand and opened the door. Duncan continued to yell orders to the driver while pointing the firearm with his right hand and holding on to the exterior door handle with his left.

     Officer Duncan states that he stepped closer to the driver until he (Duncan) was within the doorway of the Yukon but continued to grasp the exterior door handle. Up until this point, the

Yukon had been stationary but now the Yukon "jerked back" according to Officer Duncan and he heard the tires of the Yukon make a sound he described as spinning on loose gravel.

Officer Duncan states that the backward movement of the vehicle caused the open driver's door to strike him, forcing him to move ("hop") laterally with the vehicle for a distance of approximately five feet. During this time, Duncan maintained his grasp of the exterior door handle and continued to order the driver to stop. Officer Duncan states that he feared he would fall under the wheels of the Yukon or be pinned between the Yukon and the police vehicle. He also states that he did not know where Officer Brundage was and feared that Brundage could be run over or crushed between the vehicles.

Ostensibly fearing for the life of Officer Brundage as well as his own, Officer Duncan fired his Glock pistol twice from a distance he estimated to be three feet. Both shots hit the driver in the left arm and side but Duncan saw no immediate signs of compliance. The driver apparently put the Yukon into neutral or park at about this time and stiffened up in the seat resulting in the driver's foot pressing the accelerator pedal. This caused the Yukon's engine to rev loudly but the vehicle remained stationary.

Officer Duncan states that within seconds of the shooting, Officer Brundage appeared beside him to the left. As the Yukon's engine raced loudly, Duncan says that he grabbed Brundage and both jumped back from the vehicle's open door. Momentarily, Duncan realized the vehicle was not moving and the driver was not complying with his commands. Duncan states that he holstered his weapon and lunged toward the driver, grabbing the driver and removing him from the vehicle.

The driver was immediately taken to the pavement, handcuffed by the officers and his physical condition was checked. Upon discovering the driver was not breathing, officers started CPR with Officer Duncan doing respirations. This effort continued until the arrival of EMS. Shortly thereafter the driver, later identified as Antonio Scott, was pronounced dead at the scene. Officer Duncan was uninjured.

Inside the Yukon on the front passenger's seat was found what appeared to be a semiautomatic pistol. It was later determined to be a B-B gun. Officer Duncan had not seen the B-B gun before or during the incident.

Because Officer Brundage was engaged in a foot pursuit of the Yukon passenger, he witnessed none of the actual shooting. Upon hearing the shots, however, Brundage immediately looked and ran back toward the Yukon. He observed Duncan standing within the driver's door of the Yukon and heard him yelling at the driver to get out of the car. The best known witness is Ms. F. Williams who was seated in a parked compact car on the right side of the Yukon during the entire event. Ms. Williams stated that she heard the officer (Duncan) tell the driver of the Yukon numerous times to get out of the vehicle. She said that during that time, the Yukon was rolling backward and revving loudly. She reports that the officer held the gun with two hands and that four shots were fired.

Officer Duncan's statement concerning the shooting is largely corroborated by the witnesses mentioned above and by the physical evidence on scene with two potential exceptions. One is the tire marks found on the scene, the other is the conclusion of the F.D.L.E. lab that Antonio Scott's shirt showed no firearm discharge residue.

TPD homicide detectives and an accident reconstructionist took the Yukon back to the scene of the shooting to determine the origin of tire marks left by the Yukon at the time of this incident. They collectively concluded that the tire marks were caused not by the Yukon in rapid reverse acceleration, but by the Yukon in forward motion braking abruptly. The significance is that the reverse movement of the Yukon described by Officer Duncan, including the "tires spinning rapidly" on gravel sound, was not of a nature as to leave tire marks on the parking lot surface. This fact is not altogether inconsistent with Officer Duncan's statement. He acknowledges the vehicle moved only a short distance (five feet), that he was able to move with the vehicle, and that he was not injured by contact with the Yukon's door. Altogether the witness statements and the physical evidence tend to support the conclusion that the Yukon was moving backwards, but not violently so, at the time of the shooting.

Of greater concern is the F.D.L.E. lab report reflecting that the T-shirt worn by Mr. Scott at the time of the shooting "displayed six (6) holes which were examined visually, microscopically, and chemically for the presence of close range firearm discharge residues and none were found." The six holes are so situated as to be consistent with the passage of two projectiles, but the lack of discharge residue from shots fired at the distance described by Officer Duncan raises doubt as to whether Duncan truly was within the doorway of the Yukon at the time of the shooting as he says.

F.D.L.E. declined to do any distance analysis in this case so all relevant pieces of evidence, as well as report and photograph copies, were sent to the F.B.I. lab in Washington, D.C. Upon completion of testing, the F.B.I. lab reported that firearm discharge residues were present in their testing (using Officer Duncan's actual firearm) as far back from the target as seven (7) feet.

I contacted the F.B.I. lab analyst who performed the testing to determine whether the test result conclusively established that the muzzle of Officer Duncan's firearm was at least seven feet from Mr. Scott when discharged. I was informed that the test could not be said to have established that proposition. The analyst explained that firearm discharge residue typically consists of unconsumed gunpowder granules and vaporous lead. The gunpowder granules are not generally embedded in the target material and are prone to being dislodged by rough handling of the material. In this particular case, after the shooting Mr. Scott was forcibly removed from the vehicle to the pavement where he was placed face down, handcuffed, and then rolled onto his back. CPR was administered by police officers and EMS personnel who apparently cut the shirt away from Mr. Scott in their efforts to revive him. It is certainly possible that any initially attached gunpowder residue was lost during these efforts. Vaporous lead is frequently found, even when jacketed bullets are utilized, and is a much more durable residue. However, the likelihood of finding vaporous lead diminishes dramatically at distances beyond two feet. Accordingly, the lack of vaporous lead would not conclusively establish that Officer Duncan was outside of the Yukon doorway at the time of the shooting.

The policy of the Tampa Police Department regarding the use of deadly force is exceptionally strict. The general philosophy appears in SOP 536 (III) (E):

> Any action taken by an officer in self-defense or in defense of others, up to and including the death of the assailant, or any action taken by an officer in apprehending a suspect, will be considered warranted and justified if there is sufficient cause, as would appear real and reasonable to a prudent police officer, to fear the life or safety of the officer or another, or providing each of the following factors is present, given the special circumstances at hand:
>
> 1)  The police officer is acting officially within the boundaries of legal authority and established department policies and procedures;
>
> 2)  The means and the force employed are not such as a prudent officer would consider excessive, unreasonable, or unnecessary and is within the law and established department policies and procedures; and
>
> 3)  The use of firearms is within the guidelines set forth in current policies and procedures.

Regulation 1602 provides: "Department employees shall not use excessive force in making an arrest or in dealing with a prisoner or any other person."

The more specific mandates appear in SOP 537:

> Police officers are authorized to use deadly force when the officer reasonably believes that such force is necessary to:
>
> 1.  Prevent immediate death or great bodily harm to the police officer;
>
> 2.  Prevent immediate death or great bodily harm to another human being; or

3.  Apprehend the perpetrator of a felony which involved the use or threatened use of deadly force and the individual who is sought poses a threat of immediate death or great bodily harm to the police officer or another person.

The SOP goes on to provide at V.B.6: "Any doubt as to the justification for the use of deadly force must be resolved in favor of not using deadly force."

In this particular case, Officer Duncan's justification for using deadly force depends exclusively on whether he reasonably feared death or great bodily harm from the movement of the Yukon. The physical evidence does not particularly support the officer, but does not conclusively establish that the shooting was unreasonable. By Duncan's own testimony, the Yukon moved only a short distance, five feet. He was not bruised or otherwise injured by his bodily contact with the door. He was able to keep up with the Yukon without falling by hopping laterally while holding on to the exterior door handle. That he was even within the doorway of the Yukon at the time of the shooting is supported only by his own testimony. The lack of firearm discharge residue suggests otherwise but not conclusively so. There being insufficient conclusive evidence to place Officer Duncan other than where he testifies he was standing, the policy requires a consideration of whether being inside the doorway of the moving Yukon under the control of a felony suspect ignoring orders to stop could have caused a reasonable officer to fear for his life. My considered opinion is that such circumstances could cause a reasonable officer to fear immediate death or great bodily harm. As to the use of deadly force, therefore, the disposition of this investigation required by policy must be no violation.

Independent of the shooting is the issue of whether the stop of the Yukon occurred in conformance with SOP 831: Vehicle Stops – Felony/High Risk. Officer Duncan recognized that he was dealing with a probable stolen vehicle and a felony car stop. Both officers testified that Mr. Scott turned into the parking lot of his own accord and not in response to a direct order to do so inasmuch as the police vehicle was not displaying emergency lights when the Yukon stopped. The officers did not, therefore, violate the provision of SOP 831 requiring felony stops to be conducted by at least two police vehicles.

SOP 831 also requires "Both officers (two officer unit) remain at the cover position of their patrol car until all occupants are removed." Particularly in a stolen vehicle situation, when the suspects bolt from the vehicle the felony car stop is transformed into a foot pursuit. Here, the Yukon passenger ran and the officers did not know who, if anyone, remained inside. Officer Duncan wisely chose to continue to treat the Yukon as if one or more suspects remained inside but then violated SOP 831 by giving up his cover position and approaching the vehicle on foot. Had the gun on the front seat of the Yukon been real and Mr. Scott inclined to use it, Officer Duncan might well have sacrificed his life in an effort to save an insurance company a few thousand dollars. Violation of SOP 831 is sustained.

KCR/jc

# Appendix B

UNITED STATES DISTRICT COURT
MIDDLE DISTRICT OF FLORIDA
TAMPA DIVISION

BARBARA ORBAN,

 Plaintiff,

v.          CASE NO.: 8:04-CV-1904-T-23MA

CITY OF TAMPA, FLORIDA,

 Defendant.

_____/

## SETTLEMENT PROPOSAL

In order to foster settlement efforts Dr. Barbara Orban has taken the declaratory relief requested under the claims for relief and offers suggested approaches for accomplishing that relief without requiring the City to agree to liability. Therefore, we will list paragraphs from the declaratory relief sought followed by those suggested approaches.

Declaratory Relief Requested

1. A traffic citation should not be issues without reasonable and probable grounds to believe a violation has occurred.

2. The issuance of citations after it has been determined that issuance of a citation is inappropriate is unconstitutional and otherwise illegal.

3. A practice of allowing a supervisor to override a determination of an officer investigating at the scene is unconstitutional and otherwise illegal in the absence of facts showing the supervisor had reasonable and probable grounds to cause a citation to issue.

1

EXHIBIT
A

Settlement Proposal

a) Amend Tampa Police Policy 833 Traffic Crash Investigation on F. Types of Charges 1. Civil Infractions. The current policy should be deleted, which requires supervisor approval to not issue a citation. It should be replaced with language from Fla. Stat. 316.645, which states that a citation can be written in a crash investigation only if the officer conducts a personal investigation and has reasonable and probable grounds to conclude a traffic law was violated. The grounds should be documented on the citation and the crash report.

b) The policy can provide that a supervisor can override an officer's decision to not write a citation in a crash investigation only if the supervisor personally conducts an investigation, writes and signs the citation, and documents the contributing cause.

c) A listing or log of all complaints regarding traffic citations should be maintained by Internal Affairs and available for review by the public for a 10 year time period. At a minimum, the list should include the driver's name and driver license number; the citation date, number and type of infraction; the officer's name and badge number; and a brief statement of the driver's complaint.

d) All complaints made by a citizen or law enforcement officer regarding a traffic citation issued by an officer or required by a supervisor should be investigated consistent with Florida Stat. § 112.533, CALEA standards, and Tampa police Internal Affairs policy. The reports of such investigations are public records once investigations are complete, and documentation of such investigations should be available for all complaints listed on the log/listing noted above.

2

e) For unresolved disputes, an oversight system should be established outside the police department and their legal counsel. The city's ethics committee may be used for the purpose, or alternatively an oversight system through the City Council that would assure the police department abides by laws and policies. At present, the police department polices itself in an area it personally financially benefits from..

f) Re-train current officers and supervisors regarding new policies and revise training program accordingly.

### a. Declaratory Relief Requested

4.     Placing known erroneous entries in a citation or crash report to supply a rationale for the citation or conclusions of the crash report is unconstitutional and otherwise illegal.

### b. Settlement Proposal

a) Officers should be re-trained on the correct use of the long and short form crash reports, consistent with Florida law. This will have the initial impact of reducing the number of major crashes in Tampa as reported by the State. As a training officer, Officer Bowden did not have knowledge of when to use the long form report.

b) Traffic crash investigation policies must require accurate and complete reports, and a system should be established to review allegations of false entries on crash reports, amend false entries, and submit amendments to the state.

c) The police department should create a notification form that officers provide to drivers who receive a citation in a crash investigation. The form should provide

3

the crash report number and instructions on obtaining a copy of the report, and should notify the driver that the crash report serves as the officer's testimony if a hearing is requested. It should also provide information on how to contact the officer and the supervisor to address any questions or concerns about the report.

d) The police department will make reasonable effort to request the traffic courts not consider these hearsay reports.

### a. Declaratory Relief Requested

5.     The crash report applicable to the March 27, 2000 incident contains factual errors as set forth above.

### b. Settlement Proposal

a) Dr. Orban's report is now on microfiche, however hand entries can be requested to the report. The contributing cause as careless driving should be changed to "77 - All Other" and the space underneath the careless driving citation entry should note the citation was dismissed by a judge. The report should be amended: delete the misrepresentations that air bags deployed on both cars, change dry road to wet, change clear conditions to cloudy, change to "influenced by an intersection" rather than not. The narrative should add the actual accident circumstances, and note that the officers incorrectly used the long form report.

### a. Settlement Proposal Requested

6.     Traffic court use of crash reports to contradict the testimony of witnesses without providing said report to the parties and without appearance and authentication by the police officer is unconstitutional and otherwise illegal.

### b. Settlement Proposal

4

a) Addressed under 4c and 4d.

### a. Declaratory Relief Requested

7.    A *de facto* quota system for traffic citations is unconstitutional and otherwise illegal.

### b. Settlement Proposal

a) The practice of calculating average citations or arrests and evaluating officers who are below average should be discontinued. Using averages results in continuously increasing the average. At any time, half the officers would be less than the average such that when they work to the former average they increase the average.

b) Evaluations in traffic law enforcement should not be restricted to the number of moving violations written that were not associated with crash investigations. Instead, all related performance should be considered, which includes the number of traffic stops, crashes investigated, and non-moving violations, as well as productivity in other areas that affects that time available for traffic.

### a. Declaratory Relief Requested

8.    A system which causes citations to be issued to generate funds for the Police Pension Fund is unconstitutional and otherwise illegal.

### b. Settlement Proposal

a) The parties should either consent to authorizing the court or agree to jointly notify the Governor and Florida Attorney General that the law creates a real or apparent financial incentive for officers to increase insurance rates, as officers receive a pecuniary benefit when automobile insurance increases. This creates a

5

179

direct financial incentive to write more citations that increase insurance rates. In addition, a financial incentive exists to sustain or increase crash and claim rates since officers receive more extra benefits with any and all insurance increases. If crashes are reduced and insurance rates decrease as a consequence, officers would receive fewer benefits.

### a. Declaratory Relief Requested

9.     The practice of reducing employee or city contributions to the pension fund based upon premium tax revenues received is unconstitutional and otherwise illegal.

### b. Settlement Proposal

a)  Tampa fails to conform to Florida law. The amount of premium tax collections in the base year (1997) can be deducted from the annual plan cost with the remainder then allocated to city and employee contributions. However, premium tax collections in excess of the 1997 year cannot be used to reduce contribution rates and must be allocated to extra benefits.

b)  Each year, collections in excess of the base should be separately accounted for and allocated to extra benefits, which is currently defined as 300 hours of pensionable overtime.   When extra benefits revenues exceed extra benefit expenses, the surplus, and possibly any related investment income, should be carried to the next year. If extra benefit expenses exceed the related revenues, the additional expense should be added to the annual pension cost and then allocated to city and employee contributions.

c)  The extra benefit, which is 300 hours of pensionable overtime, should be amended. It creates a financial incentive for officers to write citations in order to

6

accrue overtime hours since off-duty traffic hearings result in two hours of overtime. Further, firefighters do not have a similar self initiated activity that generates overtime, such that the benefit structure is inequitable and advantages police officers who write citations relative to officers who do not write citations and the firefighters. Further, other methods to achieve overtime are not under the direct control of officers or firefighters, which further renders the benefit inequitable and not available to all.

### a. Declaratory Relief Requested

10.    The practice of having insurance companies contribute to police pension funds based upon a percentage of premiums collected is unconstitutional and otherwise illegal.

### b. Settlement Proposal

a)  See 8.a.

### a. Declaratory Relief Requested

11.    Also the practice and policy of keeping police officers away from court and not honoring subpoenas is unconstitutional and otherwise illegal.

### b. Settlement Proposal

a)  Amend policy to require officers to attend traffic hearings if subpoenaed by the other party and notify the Court and State Attorney of this requirement such that officers will be disciplined for failing to respond to such subpoenas even if they submit a crash report.

b)  See 4.c.

### a. Declaratory Relief Requested

7

181

12.  Refusing to give information to citizens that is required to given so the citizen can protest citations is unconstitutional and otherwise illegal.

b.  Settlement Proposal

a)  See 4c and 4d.

Respectfully submitted,

_____
JOSEPH D. MAGRI, ESQUIRE
Florida Bar No.: 0814490
MERKLE & MAGRI, P.A.
550 North Reo Street, Suite 301
Tampa, FL 33609
Tel. (813) 281-9000
Fax.: (813) 281-2223

8

# MERKLE & MAGRI, P.A.

5415 Mariner Street, Suite 103
Tampa, Florida 33609
(813) 281-9000
Clearwater (727) 441-2699
Fax (813) 281-2223
mm@merklemagri.com

July 25, 2007

Ursula Richardson, Esq.
City Attorney's Office
315 East Kennedy Blvd., 5<sup>th</sup> Floor
Tampa, Florida 33602

      RE:   Mediation August 1, 2007
      Case:  Appeal of Barbara Orban v. City of Tampa

Dear Ms. Richardson:

In light of the fact that it is the mayor who is ultimately responsible for the Police Department, Dr. Orban respectfully requests that Mayor Pam Iorio attend the above referenced mediation. Should Mayor Iorio's schedule will not permit her attendance at the mediation, it is requested that a member of her staff attend in her stead. It is more likely that the mediation could have a positive outcome for all concerned if either the Mayor or someone from her staff participates in the discussions.

Thank you for your attention to this matter.

Very truly yours,

*Angela Merkle for*

Joseph D. Magri

SIGNED IN
ATTORNEY'S ABSENCE
TO AVOID DELAY

EXHIBIT
B

# THE
# MAKHOLM
Law Group

JOHN A. MAKHOLM
WENDY A. MAKHOLM

July 26, 2007

Merkel & Magri, P.A.
Joseph D. Magri, Esq.
5415 Mariner Street
Suite 103
Tampa, FL 33609

RE: Mediation August 1, 2007
Case: Appeal of Barbara Orban v. City of Tampa
07-12635-BB

Dear Mr. Magri:

We are in receipt to your July 25, 2007 letter requesting that Mayor Iorio attend the Court Ordered Mediation on August 1, 2007. Unfortunately, the City of Tampa cannot honor you client's request. The designated representative from the City of Tampa will attend the Mediation as required and as you know from past Mediations with the City of Tampa, is routine. Rest assured that the Mayor's absence will not in any way hinder the Mediation, and that the representative present will have full settlement authority for the City of Tampa, to the degree that anyone can have settlement authority under the Charter of the City of Tampa. As always, I look forward to working with you on this case.

Sincerely,

John A. Makholm, Esquire
For the Defendant City of Tampa

/JAM

RECEIVED
JUL 2 7 2007

EXHIBIT
C

*DEFENDING THOSE WHO PROTECT US!* ℠

696 First Avenue North ■ Suite 205 ■ St. Petersburg, Florida 33701-3610
727.823.5100 ■ Fax 727.823.5114 ■ Email makholm@att.net / makholmw@verizon.net

# APPENDIX C

**GAO**
Accountability · Integrity · Reliability

United States Government Accountability Office
Washington, DC 20548

July 28, 2005

The Honorable Michael G. Oxley
Chairman
Committee on Financial Services
House of Representatives

Subject: *Ultimate Effects of McCarran-Ferguson Federal Antitrust Exemption on Insurer Activity are Unclear*

This letter transmits to you our briefing slides describing the potential effects of the federal antitrust exemption included in the McCarran-Ferguson Act (McCarran)[1] on insurer activities. On May 26, 2005, we briefed committee staff on the results of our review. Specifically, we assessed existing insurance practices that might violate federal antitrust law absent the McCarran exemption and identified current state authorities related to antitrust laws applicable to insurance. In a separate GAO legal opinion, *Legal Principles Defining the Scope of the Federal Antitrust Exemption for Insurance*, published in March 2005, we assessed the types of insurance-related activities that courts have found to be exempt from federal antitrust provisions under the McCarran exemption.[2]

We focused our analysis on property/casualty insurance, including workers compensation, because insurers in these areas participate in many joint activities. We consulted relevant literature, including prior congressional and state hearings on the topic, and met with experts from state insurance departments, attorneys general offices, insurance companies, trade associations, rating organizations, law firms, and academia. We met with knowledgeable staff at the National Association of Insurance Commissioners, the Department of Justice, and the Federal Trade Commission. We limited our review of states' insurance regulation and antitrust authorities to five states with large insurance markets that had varying degrees of rate regulation and differences in state antitrust exemptions—California, Illinois, New Jersey, New York, and Texas. We conducted our work from February 2005 through July 2005 in accordance with generally accepted government auditing standards.

---

[1]Pub. L. No. 79-15, ch. 20, 59 Stat. 33, codified as amended at 15 U.S.C. §§ 1011-1015.

[2]GAO, *Legal Principles Defining the Scope of the Federal Antitrust Exemption for Insurance*, B-304474 (Washington, DC: March 4, 2005).

## Background

Congress passed the McCarran-Ferguson Act (McCarran) in 1945, following a Supreme Court decision that determined that insurance is interstate commerce which Congress could regulate and subject to federal antitrust laws.[3] McCarran reaffirmed the power of the states to regulate and tax insurance companies and exempted certain insurance practices from federal antitrust laws, including the Sherman, Clayton, and Federal Trade Commission Acts. The insurance exemption applies to those activities that (a) constitute the "business of insurance;" (b) are "regulated by State law;" and (c) do not constitute an agreement or act "to boycott, coerce, or intimidate." Our legal opinion discusses court decisions concerning the types of activities covered by the exemption. Among other things, the courts have found that, generally speaking, joint rate-making among property/casualty insurers is the "business of insurance" and thus exempt from federal antitrust laws under McCarran.

Besides McCarran, there are other, more general sources of immunity from federal antitrust laws, including the *state action doctrine* and the *Noerr-Pennington Doctrine*. The *state action doctrine* allows for anticompetitive conduct provided that the conduct is both (a) part of a clearly articulated policy by a state to displace competition in a regulated area and (b) actively supervised by state regulators with statutory authority to review the conduct. The *Noerr-Pennington Doctrine* provides immunity for certain joint efforts by competitors to petition the government. Both of these immunities may be applicable to insurance. States also have their own antitrust authorities, which may or may not include exemptions for insurance.

## Effects of McCarran Exemption Uncertain, but without the Exemption Some Insurer Activities Could Raise Antitrust Concerns

Because the courts have not considered which activities within the "business of insurance" might violate federal antitrust laws, it is difficult to determine which insurer activities would withstand antitrust scrutiny if the exemption were removed. Decisions involving antitrust law are typically based on the facts and circumstances of each case. With insurance activities, if the court decides that the McCarran exemption applies, it generally conducts no further analysis of the activities. Unsure about how courts would decide insurance cases, when eliminating or proposing to eliminate antitrust immunities, legislators at both the state and federal levels have included "safe harbors" for certain insurance activities such as the collection of historical data.[4]

Some experts have suggested that absent the McCarran exemption, activities in the property/casualty area, especially joint rate-making, might violate federal antitrust

---

[3] *See United States v. Southeastern-Underwriters Ass'n*, 322 U.S. 533 (1944).

[4] California's Proposition 103, codified at Cal. Ins. Code §§ 1861 *et seq.*, had "safe harbors" embedded in its repeal of the state antitrust exemption for insurance, and congressional proposals to modify the McCarran exemption under the Insurance Competitive Pricing Act of 1994, H.R. 9, as amended, 103d Congress (1994), also carved out certain activities to avoid further litigation in these areas.

laws, citing concerns over the collective projection of insurer losses into the future. To price insurance policies, property/casualty insurers need to project loss costs—the amount insurers use to cover claims and the costs of adjusting those claims—into the future. Projecting loss costs requires large amounts of data on historical losses and actuarial expertise, and single insurers are not likely to have sufficient data or expertise in all of the insurance lines they sell. Thus, for a significant portion of rate-making, property/casualty insurers rely on rating organizations.[5] Rating organizations standardize risk classifications and products to facilitate the gathering and aggregation of data on past losses and their costs. Then, they bring this historical data up to the present by estimating loss costs for events that have occurred but have not yet been reported. Finally, rating organizations issue "advisory prospective loss costs" by projecting loss costs into the future. They do this by trending—analyzing past data trends and using actuarial judgment about the future.

According to industry representatives, regulators, and other experts, this rate-making process has certain benefits, but also raises antitrust concerns. Generally, they believe the process reduces the costs associated with pricing and regulating insurance, makes it easier for new firms to enter the insurance market, and allows consumers to better compare products. However, some experts believe that under some circumstances joint trending might constitute price fixing absent the McCarran exemption, and that standardized risk classifications and products might restrict new insurers or products from entering the market, thus limiting innovation, consumer choice, and competition. Further, according to most experts, courts are more likely to find joint trending a violation of federal antitrust laws than the joint collection of historical data.

For some, the McCarran exemption raises the issue of insurance industry uniqueness—that is, whether insurance warrants a federal antitrust exemption that most other industries do not have. Some industry representatives said that insurance is different from other industries because when it is sold the insurer does not know what the cost of a policy will be. In addition, insurer insolvencies can pose significant social costs. Some state regulators told us that lack of certainty about future costs leads some insurers to underestimate their future costs and significantly underprice their policies, potentially leading to costly insolvencies. They said that joint rate-making provides more information and greater certainty to insurers. Other experts have suggested that insurance is not unique and that other industries—such as banking—face uncertainty about future costs, but do not have antitrust immunity.

---

[5]States authorize rating organizations, sometimes called statistical or advisory organizations, to assist in the rate-making process. Nationally, two of the largest rating organizations are the Insurance Services Office in personal and commercial lines and National Council on Compensation Insurance in workers compensation.

## Application of State Antitrust Authorities to Insurance Varied Across the Five States We Visited

Although insurance is immune from federal antitrust laws, insurers in the states we visited were subject to state antitrust and related authorities to varying extents. In New York, property/casualty insurers' rate-making activities are exempt from the state antitrust laws, but the insurance code prohibits insurers from participating in unfair methods of competition. In Texas, where certain other regulated industries have exemptions, insurance has no general antitrust immunity. California and New Jersey both had periods of time in the late 1980s and 1990s when they prohibited insurers from joint trending in some lines of insurance.[6] However, state officials do not view these periods as valid experiments of how an insurance market would behave absent McCarran because of other factors influencing the market at that time. In addition, we also found that all five states had some provisions in their codes to prohibit insurers from engaging in unfair or deceptive acts or practices in their states. The states we visited also regulated property/casualty insurance rates to varying degrees. For example, California requires prior approval for many of its rates, while Illinois relies on the market to determine most rates. The degree of state rate regulation could have significant effects on the applicability of federal antitrust laws to insurance if the McCarran exemption were amended or repealed. In those states that actively regulate and enforce rates, insurers might seek and might be granted immunity from federal antitrust laws under the *state action doctrine* in the absence of the McCarran exemption.

As agreed with your office, unless you publicly announce its contents earlier, we plan no further distribution of this report until 30 days after its date. At that time, we will send copies of this report to the Chairman and Ranking Minority Member of the Senate Committee on Banking, Housing, and Urban Affairs and the Ranking Minority Member of the House Committee on Financial Services. We will also make copies of this report available to other interested parties and others upon request. In addition, it will be available on GAO's home page at http://www.gao.gov. If you or your staff have questions regarding this report, please contact me at (202)-512-8678 or hillmanr@gao.gov. Contact points for our Offices of Congressional Relations and Public Affairs may be found on the last page of this report. Lawrence D. Cluff, Nancy S. Barry, Katherine C. Bittinger, and Tania L. Calhoun made key contributions to this report.

Sincerely yours,

Richard J. Hillman
Director, Financial Markets and Community Investment

Enclosure

---

[6] In New Jersey, the state passed legislative changes only for the personal auto market.